Eleonora Rohland

# Entangled Histories and the Environment?

## Socio-Environmental Transformations in the Caribbean, 1492-1800

# Inter-American Studies
## Cultures – Societies – History

# Estudios Interamericanos
## Culturas – Sociedades – Historia

Volume 33

Eleonora Rohland

# Entangled Histories and the Environment?

## Socio-Environmental Transformations in the Caribbean, 1492-1800

WVT Wissenschaftlicher Verlag Trier
Copublished by
UNO University of New Orleans Press

**Entangled Histories and the Environment?**
**Socio-Environmental Transformations in the Caribbean, 1492-1800 /**
Eleonora Rohland. –
(Inter-American Studies | Estudios Interamericanos; 33)
Trier: WVT Wissenschaftlicher Verlag Trier, 2021
ISBN 978-3-86821-833-6
New Orleans, LA: University of New Orleans Press, 2021
ISBN 978-1-60801-208-4

SPONSORED BY THE
Federal Ministry
of Education
and Research

The project, on which this book is based, has been funded by the German Federal Ministry of Education and Research (Bundesministerium für Bildung und Forschung, BMBF). The responsibility for the content of this publication lies with the author.

Cover Image: *Novissima et Accuratissima Totius Americae Descriptio*,
Nicholas Janzoon Visscher (1658)

Cover Design: Brigitta Disseldorf

Library of Congress Cataloging-in-Publication Data
Names: Rohland, Eleonora, author.
Title: Entangled histories and the environment? : socio-environmental transformations in the Caribbean, 1492-1800 / Eleonora Rohland.
Description: New Orleans, LA : University of New Orleans Press ; Trier, Germany : Wissenschaftlicher Verlag Trier, 2021. | Series: Inter-American studies : cultures - societies - history = Estudios interamericanos : cultures - sociedades - historia ; Volume 33 | Includes bibliographical references.
Identifiers: LCCN 2020044534 | ISBN 9781608012084 (paperback)
Subjects: LCSH: Human ecology--Caribbean Area--History. | Caribbean Area--Environmental conditions.
Classification: LCC GF13.3.C27 R45 2021 | DDC 304.209729--dc23
LC record available at https://lccn.loc.gov/2020044534



Publisher: WVT Wissenschaftlicher Verlag Trier, Postfach 4005, D-54230 Trier,
Bergstraße 27, D-54295 Trier, Tel. 0049 651 41503, Fax 41504, www.wvttrier.de, wvt@wvttrier.de

Copublisher: University of New Orleans Press, 2000 Lakeshore Drive, Earl K. Long Library,
Room 221, New Orleans, LA 70148, United States, 504-280-7457, unopress.org

## Table of Contents

## 1. Preface and Introduction – or: Normalizing Environmental History in the Anthropocene

Part of the (hi-)story that will unfold over these pages started on a roof top terrace in Seville on a sweltering September afternoon in 2017. I was having a three-o'clock lunch with Heidi Scott, a historical geographer from the University of Massachusetts Amherst who was, like me, doing research on the environmental history of colonial Latin America at the Archivo de Indias. Over our late-afternoon, post-archival tapas, we got into a long conversation about the difficulty of teaching the field we were both researching, and Heidi suggested organizing a roundtable discussion on Teaching the Environmental History of the Colonial Americas for the annual conference of the American Historical Association (AHA) 2019. And so, at the end of the first week of January 2019, Heidi, Gregory Cushman, Daviken Studnicki-Gizbert, Cameron Strang and I were discussing this theme at the AHA conference in Chicago. Among many other important points, we agreed that environmental history still needed to be normalized.[1] That is, despite the fact that environmental history is an established field – at least in the U.S. and many Latin American countries, less so in Germany – it is still a field that stands out and is treated apart from "normal," i.e. political, social, and cultural history. However, since environmental and climatic questions have affected human societies in various and often adverse ways throughout history and into the present, a goal, we agreed, would be to integrate environmental history to such an extent that it becomes normal to teach students the environmental effects of war, or the influence of climate and disease on early colonial settlers without having to add an environmental history tag to the course. That is, in short, to close the nature-culture gap in the way we teach history.

A second strand of this (hi-)story pre-dates the Sevillean Tapas-eating by two years and begins in cold and rainy Germany, at

---

1 I thank all four scholars for the inspiring conversations before, during, and after our roundtable.

Bielefeld University. Bielefeld's Latin American history department has been hosting an interdisciplinary research project entitled "The Americas as a Space of Entanglements," which is linked to a long-standing Bielefeldian tradition of exploring entanglements in the global South, the "Bielefelder Verflechtungsansatz" developed throughout the 1980s (Evers 1986). The context of this project and discussions with my colleagues compelled me to think more intensely and systematically about entanglements/entangled histories in the context of my own new book project on socio-environmental transformation in the colonial Caribbean. The initial experience when working through the research literature on entanglements/entangled histories and post-colonial criticism was, yet again, that of staring squarely into the abyss of the nature-culture divide. So, the resulting vertigo became the spur for wanting to integrate "nature" and "the environment" into the concept of entanglement, ideas that I will outline a little further below.

The third strand of this (hi-)story refers to the discourse and research about the Anthropocene. It's an often-stated truism that historians are children of their time and so their questions and focus are influenced by the current events of their time as well. This study is no exception, and as may be evident, the first two strands mentioned above are closely connected or even encompassed by this third. The "Anthropocene" has been discussed as a new geological epoch in which humans have become a planetary-scale force in changing the globe from its deep soil layers and the oceans to the higher atmosphere. It was proposed by Dutch atmospheric chemist and Nobel Laureate Paul Crutzen and by U.S. biologist Eugene Stoermer in 2000 (Crutzen and Stoermer 2000). The two researchers suggested the new term to contrast with the still-ongoing Holocene, which Geologists are dating, with the help of Greenland ice cores, from 11'700 years ago (Walker et al. 2009). This is the era during which the Neolithic Revolution took place and during which human civilizations as we know them today have developed. This latter fact is largely due to the relatively mild climatic conditions that have persisted throughout the Holocene and that have allowed humans to expand and thrive in all climatic zones of the globe. Humans – particularly those living in the Global North, but some parts of the Global South are following suit – are currently jeopardizing this situation by putting unprecedented amounts of $CO_2$ into the atmosphere through their mass-use of fossil fuels, by the extraction of non-renewable resources, by industrial patterns of land use, by the pollution of soils and oceans through plastic, and by the mass-extinction of other species, to mention just a few aspects that constitute the concept (Mauelshagen, 2017a, 2017b; Steffen, Grinevald, Crutzen, and McNeill 2011). The debates that have unfolded in the humanities, social, and natural sciences over the last decade or so, and more intensely over the last five years, focus on the dating points of this new epoch (the natural sciences and a few historians) on the one hand, and on the term "Anthropocene" (the humanities) on the other hand. These are central issues that I will however not elaborate on here. Rather, I would like to point to a third theme that refers back to the feeling of vertigo over the nature-culture divide mentioned above and that touches the heart of the historical discipline as it has evolved since the end of the nineteenth century.

In his seminal 2009 article on "The Climate of History", Dipesh Chakrabarty explained how the fact that humans were now changing the climate (and other planetary systems) spelt the end of the separation between human and natural history.

> Humans have become geological agents very recently in human history. In that sense, we can say that it is only very recently that the distinction between human and natural histories – much of which had been preserved even in environmental histories that saw the two entities in interaction – has begun to collapse. For it is no longer a question simply of man having an interactive relation with nature. This, humans have always had, or at least that is how man has been imagined in a large part of what is generally called the Western tradition. Now it is being claimed that humans are a force of nature in the geological sense. A fundamental assumption of Western (and now universal) political thought has come undone in this crisis. (Chakrabarty 2009, 207)

In an acutely tangible and material form, the Anthropocene brings home the realization how deeply entangled human societies have been with their environments, even throughout the fossil and the atomic age with their illusion of the separation of human societies from planetary energy limits (Mauelshagen 2020).[2] Chakrabarty also notes that the field of environmental history has built on the understanding of humans as biological agents – a perspective that remains largely confined to that field, while "general" history has understood humans almost exclusively as social agents – but not as biological or even geological ones, that is, as a planet-altering force. Historian Franz Mauelshagen has described this paradigmatic shift in terms of earth system sciences, as humans moving beyond the biosphere, where they have dwelled throughout the Holocene (Mauelshagen 2019). Given these spatially large-scale and temporally deep-time shifts in human interactions with their surroundings it seems a new, integrative perspective on history is in order that does not relegate "the environment" to a sub-field of history, that, at least in the German historical context is treated like a curious but not quite to-be-taken-seriously addition to "real" (i.e. political, social and cultural) history. Which brings me back to strands one and two of this story, the aim of normalizing environmental history and to including the environment into the concept of entangled histories. While I do not claim that including environmental factors into entanglement will be *the* solution to the challenge of the Anthropocene to the historical discipline, I would like to offer some considerations on this link, as *one way* of acquiring a new perspective.

One might wonder why, of all things, a so far relatively under-theorized concept as entanglement/entangled histories should be considered part of the solution to such large-scale disciplinary questions that, frankly, have been around for ages. There are two an-

2 I explicitly use the term "human societies" to encompass all societies and not differentiating between societies of the global north and south, since even western development policies – and in Latin America the neo-extractivist developmental model – are based on the massive exploitation of non-renewable energy sources.

swers to this understandable doubt: On the one hand, the simple solutions are often the most elegant and widely accessible, and on the other hand, the concept of entangled history has emerged from an engagement of post-colonial critics with a discourse on comparative, transnational and global histories. It already includes, or is at least open to, an intersectional perspective that is crucial when considering the environmental problems of the Anthropocene, but that is equally crucial when considering historical processes in the colonial context where the historical record is generally skewed towards the white European male perspective. This is particularly true for the Inter-American and specific Caribbean focus of this study, a region with ecologically sensitive island ecosystems, climatic and other extreme events and histories of extreme domination and violence by European colonial powers towards indigenous men and women in particular and towards enslaved African men and, again, women in particular.

In historical (and other) research, the term "entanglement" is often loosely and metaphorically used to describe processes of interaction or connection. However, "entanglement" has acquired a more specific meaning within a scholarly debate during the first decade of the 21$^{st}$ century (Epple and Lindner 2011, Kaltmeier, Lindner, and Mailaparambil 2011). Anthropologist and Sociologist Shalini Randeria's proposition to speak of "entangled histories and uneven modernities" in postcolonial contexts, rather than of collective-singular "history" and "modernity" with the model being European or western, arose from the debate about transnational, global, and comparative history mentioned above.

In the U.S. this discussion had started with Ian Tyrell's call to look beyond American exceptionalism in 1991, and in Germany a decade later with Matthias Middell and Jürgen Kocka's publications in 2000 and 2001 (Tyrrell 1991, Middell 2000, Kocka 2001). Comparative history and its most frequent object, cultural transfer, were criticized for being Eurocentric, essentializing, treating nations as closed containers, and transfer as being thought of as if it was a unidirectional process, that, in the (post)colonial context usually went from "metropole" to "periphery." The same had been criticized earlier by early modern South Asian historian Sanjay Subrahmanyam who suggested that "we not only compare from within our boxes, but spend some time and effort to transcend them, not by comparison alone, but by seeking out the at times fragile threads that connected the globe [...]," and thus what he called "connected histories" (Subrahmanyam 1997). Within the European debate, and French-German relations in particular, historians Bénédicte Zimmermann and Michael Werner developed the approach of *histoire croisée* – entangled history – in order to overcome these problems (Werner and Zimmermann 2002, 2006). Randeria's "entangled histories of uneven modernities" then took entangled history one step further, away from its still Europe-centered focus.

However, the common thread to all these subfields of history and literary studies that engaged in the discourse about global and transnational history, comparison, and modernity(-ies) was that their thematic focus was centered on political, social, cultural and in rather fewer cases, economic factors, while "the environment" or "nature" remained a separate issue relegated to environmental history. In the U.S., the field of environmental history actually predated the debate on transnational history by almost a decade with Donald Worster's call for "the internationalizing of environmental history" in 1982 (Worster 1982). The next landmark environmental history publication that engaged in the discourse of transnational perspectives was Richard White's "Nationalization of Nature" in the Journal of American History in 1999 (White 1999). And while environmental historians of countries of the Global South have readily adopted theoretical and conceptual approaches from post-colonial studies, their work, and the significance of environmental factors for the making of colonial empires and post-colonial unequal relationships of power has not found their way back into that field nearly in the same measure.

As a consequence of these separate strands of disciplinary development, Entangled history, or *Verflechtungsgeschichte*, has largely focused on the nation state and transnational relations, on entanglements of cultures, the uneven distribution of social and political power, and – where it is based on development and dependence theories – on economic aspects influencing such power (Kay 1989, Wallerstein 1974). That is, "entanglement" was focused on structures of power distribution between people, but not on how the access to, and use of, natural resources, land, and energy was often the foundation of such power and its unequal distribution. For the field of history, this is rather surprising since the obvious place of environmental factors in transnational and colonial history was described in the works of well-known environmental historians Alfred Crosby (Crosby 1986, 1972), Richard Grove (Grove 1996) and John McNeill (McNeill 2010). In other words, it seems that thinking about the environment ("nature") as an integral component of colonial history (but mostly not under the perspective of entanglements) remains largely confined to the subfield of environmental history, while the proponents of Entangled history and post-colonial critics in the field of literature largely continue blanking out "nature" in their studies of uneven power relations.[3]

The Caribbean as the geographical focus of this study and of the so-far outlined approach to entanglement/entangled histories may create all sorts of "been there – done that" reactions. In particular with regard to Crosby's "Columbian Exchange" mentioned above and with regard to the subject of the evolution of the plantation system, two of the best-researched subjects when it comes to environmental histories of the Caribbean (Crosby 1972; Funes Monzote 2008; McCook 2002, 2011). However, the approach I am outlining below and throughout the two case studies neither focuses on the circulation of plants, animals, pathogens and humans nor exclusively on the specific environment of the plantation. Rather, my argument is of a more systemic nature. Entanglement that includes these factors can be exemplified exceptionally well on the geographical region of the Caribbean. The archipelago is something like a "knot" in entangled histories, to remain in the metaphor.

3 This "false divide between environmental history and the criticism of empire" has recently been pointed out along very similar lines by literary scholars Nathan Hensley and Philip Steer (Hensley and Steer 2019, 5-6).

During the period of research that I am focusing on in this essay, the Caribbean was a veritable colonial microcosm, successively – and sometimes simultaneously – claimed by more and less important European trading powers: Spain, England, France, the Netherlands, later also Denmark, Sweden and the United States. The transatlantic slave trade as a central component of the agrarian organization of labor and of the functioning of the plantation system linked the entanglement with Africa. Even though the socio-environmental entanglement of forced agrarian labor makes the nature-culture divide less tangible in the history of slavery, the vast majority of research on enslaved Africans in the Americas focuses on the social, juridical, material, or gender aspects of the trade and the people that were traded (Bennett 2019; Block 2018; Borucki, Eltis, and Wheat 2015; Curran 2011; Eltis 1997; Eltis, Lewis, and McIntyre 2010; Klein and Vinson 2007; Newman 2018; Schiebinger 2017; Seth 2014, 2018). A very small subfield of this research is concerned with the environmental and subsistence conditions of enslaved Africans on different Islands of the Caribbean (e.g. Mandelblatt 2008, 2013, 2016; Sheridan 1976; Watts 1984).

As stated above, "entanglement" is often used metaphorically, without clarifying what creates these uneven power structures, or, phrased differently, without stating what the *factors of entanglement* actually are. These factors, or key aspects of entanglement are relatively straight-forward and no great news for historians of the Atlantic World. In the following few paragraphs, I will nevertheless briefly summarize these key factors since they are the basis for my argument about the place of the environment or "nature" in entangled history(ies).

*Colonial political power* is a first key to the History of Entanglement in the Americas without which neither the transformation of the social sphere nor the transformation of the environment can be understood. From the end of the sixteenth century onwards, the Caribbean became the center of the transatlantic slave trade until Brazil took over this role in the nineteenth century. The sheer scale of this trade and the role of the Caribbean in particular has been visualized by the maps published in David Eltis and David Richardson's Atlas on the transatlantic slave trade (Eltis and Richardson 2010; Eltis and Halbert 2013).

With regard to Entangled history, *colonial migration* is a – if not *the* – key factor for understanding the transformation of the social as well as the natural environment of the Americas. Apart from forced migration, colonial migration also includes the migration from Europe, and inter-American migration. These movements of people have shaped the composition and the dynamic change of societies across the western hemisphere. This process of societal change has been subsumed under the term "creolization." Both, the terms *mestizo* as well as *creole* already appear in records from the second half of the sixteenth century. As Early Modern Latin American historian Rebecca Earle recently remarked in her book *The Body of the Conquistador*, "it was the importance ascribed to environment (understood in the broadest sense to include the region's climate, its waters and foods and the stars that governed it) that explains the evolution in the colonial era of the idea of the 'creole' – someone of European heritage born in the Indies" (Earle 2012). In other words, in the perception of contemporaries, societal transformation was not merely a function of a new mix of colonial migrant groups, but largely depended on the interaction of humans with the environment. In order to understand how societal change and environmental change were interlaced in the Americas and the Caribbean in particular, it is important to focus specifically on cultural practices. This connection and consequent entanglements will be highlighted and exemplified throughout the following case studies. Two further key factors of colonial entanglements that need to be mentioned are trade and knowledge.

The *trade* into which the (Circum-)Caribbean became involved, encompassed humans, plants, and other "goods." Spatially, this trade was increasingly organized on a supra-regional if not global scale, which made it one of the drivers of early globalization and hence of western modernity (Bayly 2004). One of the preconditions for trade was agricultural production, which emerges as the most important node for the entanglement of the four factors of entanglement: colonial power, migration, trade and knowledge. The reason for the importance of agriculture is that it is not only the node for interaction between humans or human cultures, but also for the interaction between humans, plants, animals and local climates – that is, environment in its widest sense.

The fourth factor of entanglement, lastly, is *knowledge*, specifically the kind that was involved in the conscious and intentional part of what Alfred Crosby called the Columbian Exchange. Since "knowledge" *per se* is too vast to be a meaningful analytical category in this context, the focus is in particular on the aspects of generation, acquisition, and circulation of new knowledge in the transformation of unfamiliar environments in the Caribbean and the Americas at large. The key themes in this regard are discourses on crops, cultivation techniques, climatic extreme events and the effect of unfamiliar American climates on European bodies. These aspects are almost omnipresent in the colonial discourse. The history of knowledge connected with these aspects has to be considered in the context of local entanglements between different migrant groups as well as in the transatlantic entanglements between government and scientific institutions in the Caribbean and Europe (McClellan 2010; Bleichmar, De Vos, Huffine, and Sheehan 2009, Delbourgo and Dew 2008; Rohland 2016, 2017). It may be evident from the above, that knowledge is closely linked to the other factors of entanglement – power, migration and trade. Knowledge is, hence, not only being renewed by these factors, but, conversely, these three factors also influenced knowledge and innovation.

So much for the relatively obvious factors of entanglement. But where is the environment in all this? First of all, including environmental and climatic factors into (post-)colonial entanglements does not mean promoting a new kind of materialism, and even less, determinism. Monocausal historical explanations, no matter from which angle, have never proven robust or long-lasting. Rather – and taking overcoming the nature-human divide seriously – environmental and climatic aspects are already entwined with the other four factors and with agriculture as the central practice and node where the four factors of entanglement come together. However, the fact that the environment and climate cannot simply be added as a fifth factor makes them inherently messy from a theoretical point of view. At the same time, this is the whole point of including the environment/climate in entangled history(ies). It needs to be found and followed in each of the four factors mentioned above and, in doing so will render a more realistic reconstruction of the past than if we were to simply add it as a "bloc." Applying this rather complex analytic may also help to prevent determinism. Instead of outlining on an abstract level how environmental and climatic aspects are entwined with the four factors of entanglement mentioned above, these multiple entanglements will be exemplified in the following case studies, which may also, then, show how including the environment in the study of entanglements could be one way of normalizing environmental history. However, before diving into these case studies, a last but crucial strand for the understanding of this study's approach needs to be explained.

Just when everybody thought, comparison had breathed its last sigh, precisely *because* of the debate between historians and post-colonial critics outlined above, and because of entangled history as a solution to the problem of Eurocentrism and "othering" – Bielefeld University emerged with a large-scale interdisciplinary, inter-faculty project (SFB 1288 Practices of Comparing: Ordering and Changing the World) on Practices of Comparing. Rather than being a re-take of the old approach of using comparison as a method, as some had erroneously thought, this project explores the "doing of comparison." That is, it looks at comparison as a historically embedded practice. By so doing, its aim is to ultimately uncover the dynamic force of practices of comparing for macro-scale historical transformation processes. It is hence focusing on contexts within which comparison occurs, and on their role in processes of historical change (Albert et al. 2019; Epple 2015; Epple and Erhart 2015). Since the options here could potentially be endless, it is also the aim of the approach to identify conjunctures of comparison, phases in history where practices of comparing became particularly pertinent.

Colonial situations of cultural contact, conquest or colonization belong to these phases as I will show below and as a 2018 conference at the Center for Interdisciplinary Research (ZiF) in Bielefeld on that subject have brought to light with examples from around the globe (Rohland, Epple, Flüchter, and Kramer 2021).

This brings us back to entangled history. Scholars of the field may now frown at this attempt of bringing together entanglement and comparison, since the latter has been considered overcome by the relational approaches of entangled and connected history(ies). Yet, perceived as a context-specific, historical practice rather than using it as a methodological tool to generate historical insight, practices of comparing can be productively employed in researching entangled histories in the Americas (see also Epple 2020). In fact, I argue, and hope to show with my examples, that it makes specific sense in the context of the history of the Americas to bring the perspective of the environment-in-entanglement and practices of comparing together. Or, taking my argument one step further, that practices of comparing can become a driver for entangled histories (explicitly in the plural this time).

As may have become evident from the above, this essay has been inspired by several different and ongoing research and book projects. It represents a first synthesis of research and thoughts of the past four years and is of a somewhat programmatic character. That is, a lot of it is still work in progress so far mainly based on secondary literature and printed primary sources.

This essay contains two case studies, each of which will outline specific aspects of socio-environmental entanglement and the role of practices of comparing in the unfolding colonization of the Spanish, French and British Caribbean. Chapter 2, *Arriving*, shows what projections of "nature," of the indigenous population and of food resources the Spanish came to the island of Hispaniola (which was called Bohío, Quisqueya or Ayiti in the indigenous language of the Arawak) with, and how these ideas affected the initial, European socio-environmental entanglement on the island. The chapter follows the well-known reports on Christopher Columbus' "discovery" of Hispaniola and the following voyages to the island by the Spanish chroniclers Gonzalo Fernandez de Oviedo, Bartolomé de las Casas, and Pietro Martire d'Anghiera. In particular, we focus on Columbus' second voyage and arrival on Hispaniola to a famine that, according to the Spanish reports, was caused intentionally by the indigenous population and lasted from 1494 to 1496. The chapter offers an alternative analysis to the traditional perception of the cause of this famine, which is to accept the European reports at face value. It highlights the difficulty of understanding and comparing unfamiliar social and natural environments and climates at the turn of the fifteenth century.

The third chapter, *Extracting*, is an exploration of the cultural construction of "climate" and its role in the extractivist labor practices of the plantation system. With the appearance of the first enslaved Africans on Caribbean islands, the discourse we today subsume under the concept of "tropicality" – coined by David Arnold in 1996 (Arnold 1996a), based on Edward Said's "orientalism" (Said 1978) – started to develop. The consequences of cultural encounters of culturally heterogeneous populations were already subject to intense debate by contemporaries of the eighteenth and nineteenth centuries. Drawing on a repertory of knowledge informed by Galenic and Hippocratic medicine, early eighteenth-century scientific discussions mixed theories about the influence of climate on the human character, political regimes, and the culture of entire regions or "civilizations" (Gerbi 2010). In brief, steeped in practices of comparing, these theories all held in common that environmental conditions of the tropics had an effect on the "moral economy" of the local population. That is, that over the course of several generations an inadvertent *acclimatization* of the human character to his or her environment would occur. Chapter three thus shows how American and Caribbean slave-holding societies could hardly resist the attraction of the *topos* of moral and physical acclimatization, as the supposed "pre-adaptedness" of Africans to tropical climates became the most wide-spread argument in favor of slavery.

## 2. Arriving: Unfamiliar and Incomparable Environments on Hispaniola?

The initial strands of entanglement that make up the first contact situation between Christopher Columbus, the Spanish who accompanied him, and the Arawak[4] on the island of Hispaniola lie in the late medieval European Mediterranean. This is well-trodden historical territory, so we will only linger here very briefly in order to find the environment in the factors of entanglement laid out in the introduction. The Spanish expansion across the Atlantic was driven by the search for a western route to what Europeans considered "India" (see Wey Gómez 2008, 159-229; Schulz 2016, 175-186, 355-379) and its spices and for gold and silver, which had become increasingly rare in Europe throughout the fourteenth and early fifteenth centuries. The apparent depletion of European gold and silver mines, which had in some cases been worked since Roman times, led to a depreciation of minted coins, the value of which dropped with the vanishing content of the respective precious metal. The consequent inflation troubled the power politics of the Spanish and Portuguese monarchs at the end of the fifteenth century (Parker 1983; Reinhard 2016, 294-295). There was, in other words, a direct link between natural resources, the stability of early modern financial flows and the ability of monarchs to exert power and expand their empires by waging costly wars.

Driven by these combined economic and environmental factors as well as the competition for colonial expansion with Portugal, Columbus set out on his venture to find a western (and southern, as we will see in more detail in chapter 3) sea route to "India" in August 1492. Columbus and his fleet of three ships had first sighted land and happened upon the *Lucayos*, or what we call the Bahamas to-

4 The Greater Antilles (Cuba, Haiti, Puerto Rico, and Jamaica) were originally inhabited by the Arawak people who came to be called Arawak by 20th century anthropologists, a term which was "taken casually from the name for a single social class." I thus follow Carl O. Sauer's example in calling them Arawak throughout this essay (Sauer 1966, 37).

day, on October 11, 1492. By December 6, he had made his way to the island that its inhabitants, the Arawak, called Ayiti or Bohío and that Columbus named Hispaniola. He noted that

> This big island appeared to be very high, not encircled by mountains but level like beautiful fields. It appears to be all cultivated, or at least a large part of it, and the crops look like wheat in the month of May in the vicinity of Córdoba.
>
> It is very high, and upon the highest mountain plowing could be done with oxen and everything could be transformed into fields and pastures. In all Castile there is no land that can be compared to this beauty and fertility. All this island and the Isla de la Tortuga are entirely cultivated like the plain of Córdoba.
>
> The weather here, with respect to the breezes and temperature, is the same as it is in Castile in March.
>
> They [the Indians] have no arms and are naked, and have no knowledge of arms and are very timid. A thousand of them would not face three Christians, and so they are suitable to be governed and made to work and sow and do everything else that shall be necessary, to build villages and be taught to wear clothing and to observe our customs. (Fuson 1992, 127, 137, 142, 138)

These passages from Columbus' logbook are noteworthy in several respects. In order to convey to his readers what he was seeing, the explorer employed comparison as a rhetorical strategy. He described never-before-seen crops, climate and human beings in terms of an environment that would be familiar to them – Castile and Córdoba. Born in Genova and with experience in Portugal, Spain and part of the African West coast, those places were his horizon of experience and comparison. In addition, believing he had arrived in the Orient, he projected his expectations of the products and people he would find there onto the unfortunate Arawaks of Hispaniola and the other peoples of the Caribbean archipelago.

Columbus' logbook, like earlier Portuguese and Spanish accounts of the circumnavigation of the African coast, stands in the larger tradition of ancient travel writing and the genre of the *periplus*. The latter is defined as conveying factual descriptions of so far unknown stretches of coastal geography in order to inform other sailors and travelers of the dangers and marvels of new found lands and how to get to them (Dueck and Brodersen 2012, 52-53; Matei-Chesnoiu 2015, 26; Schulz 2016, 181-182). Whether or not Columbus actually embellished his account of Hispaniola in order to gain fame and further funding from King Ferdinand and Queen Isabella, is almost secondary to my focus here. What is much more interesting with regard to practices of comparing and entangled history is the relevance of these comparisons for concrete action and their dramatic potential to affect the course of history.

In the *Columbian Exchange*, the American environmental historian Alfred Crosby (Crosby 1972) uncovered the unprecedented and ongoing dynamics of ecological entanglement unleashed by Columbus' landing in the Caribbean and by his assumption of similarity – the basic mechanism of practices of comparing – with Mediterranean environments and climates. Based on this perceived similarity, Columbus imported animals and plants from Europe with unintended but far-reaching consequences for flora, fauna and humans in the Americas and around the globe. Travelling along as stowaways with the *intended* consequences of this comparison were the European diseases Columbus and his men unwittingly brought to the Americas. The immune systems of the indigenous peoples had never before experienced such pathogens as measles, smallpox, and flu, and they hence spelled demographic disaster for the Arawak as well as the indigenous peoples of both subcontinents that the Spaniards "discovered" in the following decades of the sixteenth century (Livi Bacci 2008; Moya Pons and Flores Paz 2013).

Columbus' comparison and explicit assumption of similarity between Castile and Hispaniola ecologically reunited the Eurasian and the American continent that had biologically evolved separately due to continental drift and the submergence of the Bering land bridge, which had last connected the two landmasses some 13'000 years before present (Crosby 1972). With regard to socio-environmental entanglement and unequal relationships of colonial power, the inadvertent effects of European pathogens in the Americas is exemplary. They were part of the reason why Europeans could dominate the Americas as they did and why Europeans were able to replace parts of the indigenous populations with enslaved Africans, more Europeans, and with Asians. No other continent to which Europeans came with the aim of colonization, except maybe Australia, experienced such a forced turnover and up-rooting of its population. While none of the above are new examples, I am mentioning them here as the most salient cases of comparative practices in the context of Entangled history and even more so in the context of environmental aspects in entangled history.

## The 1494-1496 Famine on Hispaniola – An Indigenous Conspiracy?

From setting in motion, the Columbian Exchange in 1492 by way of comparison, we fast forward to Columbus' second voyage to Hispaniola in 1494. Apart from himself, Columbus' journeys were recorded by several fifteenth- and sixteenth-century Spanish chroniclers whose accounts vary in temporal proximity to the actual events as well as with regard to the eyewitness status of the authors. Gonzalo Fernandez de Oviedo's *Historia General y Natural de las Indias* (Fernández de Oviedo y Valdés 1535), for example is a relatively "late" publication with regard to the events described, though he did use firsthand sources in addition to his own observations. Oviedo only stopped on the island in 1514, a point in time where the Arawak had already experienced Spanish violence and pathogens for 22 years. The chronicler then took up proper residence in Santo Domingo in the 1530s, which was the time when the original societal structures of the indigenous population had already been disrupted and Spanish settlers started leaving the island for more promising *Tierra Firme*.

These circumstances influenced his narrative and rather negative perception of the Arawak (Anderson-Córdova 2017, 416). It is well known that Bartolomé de las Casas has a much more positive perception of the indigenous peoples of Hispaniola, which he describes in his *Historia de las Indias* (Casas, Fuensanta del Valle, Sancho Rayón 1875 (1575)). Las Casas arrived on Hispaniola in 1502, much earlier than Oviedo, which gave him the advantage of seeing the Arawak chiefdoms at a stage when they were still-functioning socio-cultural and economic fabrics. He also had access to a large corpus of documents that later scholars were deprived of. Lastly, Pietro Martire d'Anghiera's *Decades of the new world* (d'Anghiera 1555; the first edition in Latin appeared in 1516) also provided an account of Columbus' "discovery" and subsequent voyages. As opposed to Oviedo and Las Casas, d'Anghiera, had, however, never set foot in the Americas and compiled his *Decades* from letters, accounts, and personal interviews of explorers and colonial officials who had. Many of his accounts appear to be exaggerated and, in some places, "full of rhetoric" (Anderson-Córdova 2017, 417-419; Sauer 1966, 38-39).

All three accounts mention a famine that occurred on Hispaniola between 1494 and 1496. All three European chroniclers agree that the famine was caused by a malicious ploy of the indigenous people that aimed at starving out the Spanish to cast them from the island. The research literature on the early settlement of Hispaniola (Altman 2007; Cook 1993, 2002; Deagan and Cruxent 2002; Deagan 2010; Livi Bacci 2008; Mira Caballos 1997; Sauer 1966; Wilson 1990) deals with this event in the context of the island's early demography and does not question the European narrative of the indigenous ploy to drive out the Spaniards.

This – one could almost call it a conspiracy theory – caught my attention reminding me of accounts from my research on the French settlement of Louisiana in 1699 (Margry 1881; Rohland 2019), of the archaeologist Dennis Blanton's research on the beginnings of the Jamestown Colony in 1607 (Blanton 2000), and of a colleague's research on Portuguese Expeditions to Zimbabwe in the 1570s

(Hannaford 2018; Hannaford and Nash 2016). In all of these first contact instances, European colonials mention problems with obtaining food stuffs in unfamiliar environments and their negotiations with the local population they encountered. The Portuguese and the English employed a very similar argument to what the early Spanish chroniclers tell about the Arawak of Hispaniola. European colonists, in a first instance, relied on their own provisions from Europe when setting out on Explorations into far-away parts of the earth. This was in line with their humoral pathological world view, which held that only their native crops and nourishment would sustain their health, spirits, and character optimally (Chaplin 2001; Earle 2010, 2012). Once their provisions were depleted, the next riskier and "unhealthier" option was to fall back on indigenous foodstuffs, be it by friendly exchange or violent appropriation. If the European impostors could not obtain indigenous provisions by either means, they suspected the native population of maliciously hiding the foodstuffs from them.

We know similar patterns of blaming certain social or ethnic groups from Early Modern European Famine Research. However, in these cases the density of historical records and the concrete references of contemporaries to weather phenomena make it easier to connect the famines with climatic anomalies. In other words, for early modern Europe, the entanglement of social and climatic factors can be retraced rather clearly in historical hindsight. With regard to suspicions of specific social groups tampering with food crops, in the European context bakers and merchants were often – and sometimes not without reason – suspected of driving up bread prices by hoarding corn. Hoarding was called "Fürkauf" in German. Connected with this was the image of the "Kornjude", the "corn Jew," which emerged during the 17th century in German-speaking lands, according to Wolfgang Behringer (Behringer, Lehmann and Pfister 2015, 64; Gailus 2001).

Wolfgang Behringer as well as Christian Pfister have pointed to the link between the climatic anomalies of the Little Ice Age and increases in witch burnings for "weather magic" (Behringer 2005;

Pfister 2007). In other words, even if European early modern societies understood the connections between "bad weather", crop failures, and famines very clearly, the weather, on the one hand, was still in the hands of God, and bad harvests a sign of his Wrath (Mauelshagen 2011); and on the other hand this situation led communities to seek for a local outlet for anxiety about the evolving emergency situations. Those outlets were found in the stereotyped figure of the baker, the Jewish corn merchant, or the witch.

Now, what happens if this Christian-European early modern world view is transplanted into an unfamiliar environment with an unknown climate in which there is neither an understanding for the seasonality of crop planting and growth nor for what may be – in twenty-first century terms – considered as climatically "normal" circumstances?[5] The American archaeologist Dennis Blanton asked this question in the context of the first English attempts at settling the American East Coast in the Jamestown colony from 1607 onwards (Blanton 2000). I am using his study as a best-practice case for this chapter despite the fact that it lies chronologically over a hundred years ahead of the Spanish case. The limits of this setup will become evident a little further below. Blanton was able to show that the English first contact situation with the indigenous people of the Chesapeake Bay happened during a time of extreme and long-lasting drought by combining archaeological, historical, and climatological evidence from tree rings. He uncovered the English suspicion, that the Powhatans were maliciously hiding their food from the newcomers, as a misinterpretation by the Europeans and their inability to assess the unfamiliar climate and environment. Importantly, the addition of climate as an explanatory factor for the food scarcity in 1609 and 1610 does not mean we should *a priori* dismiss the accounts of indigenous groups hiding corn from the English. Rather, it expands our understanding for their doing so, beyond the

5 Archaeologist Marcy Rockman has pointed to the fact that it takes humans about one generation (c. 35 years) to establish robust knowledge of environmental and climatic cycles in a given area they move to (Rockman 2003, 15).

"malice" trope assigned by the English contemporaries or other social factors that researchers have since ascribed as a reason.

But why has it been so difficult or unintuitive to include the environment and climate as contributing factors for the early hardship of European colonial endeavors in the Americas?[6] Blanton states that in the Jamestown case

> interpretations of the first-person accounts vary in the attribution of hardship, but none of them implicates drought as a significant factor in the first years. [...] The closest explicit mention comes from the [...] native appeal for [John] Smith to pray for rain. *Indeed, this sort of ambiguity still leads to dismissal of the environment as a significant factor in early colonial events.* (Blanton 2000, 79, emphasis added)

Blanton assigns this absence of references to the environment or climate to the inexperience of the English newcomers with the natural cycles of their new surroundings (ibid.). I would venture one step further and say that as a result of such missing environmental causality the focus of Jamestown contemporaries moved fully into the social realm.

Looking into Captain John Smith's – the founder of the Jamestown colony on the Chesapeake Bay – account of the English first contact situation on the east coast of North America, the idea of the best practice study may be biting its own proverbial tail, though in an interesting way with regard to practices of comparing. About halfway into the first volume, which tells of the English hardship and conflict with the indigenous groups of the Chesapeake Bay, Smith inserts a consideration of the birth-pains of rising states. He compares Virginia with Rome, which "grew by oppression and rose upon the backe of her enemies" and – unsurprisingly – with the Spaniards who "have had many of those counterbuffes, more than

6 It is important to note that Karen Ordahl Kupperman was among the first historians to point to climatic and environmental anxieties of the English in Jamestown, although without including paleoclimatological evidence, see Kupperman 1979, 1982, 1984, 2007.

we" (Smith, Arber and Bradley 1910, 580). Smith then gives an account of the Spanish conquest of Hispaniola, including the passage where the "Indians [...] generally conspired together to plant no more at all, intending thereby to famish [the Spaniards]; themselves in the meantime living upon Cassava, a root to make bread, only then known to themselves" (ibid.). First, the comparison with ancient Rome clearly belongs to a well-established European intellectual repertoire of practices of comparing when it comes to describing or imagining empire. What is more, the comparison with Spain, the great European empire the English were trying to emulate, reinforces the *topos* of the "treacherous Indian" that the Spanish had created. In other words, in the Jamestown case, blaming the indigenous population for their hardship may as much have been an effect of English unfamiliarity with the Chesapeake environment as comparing their own situation with that of the Spaniards in Hispaniola a century earlier.

## Incomparable Environments and the Creation of an Urban Myth

So, back to Columbus and the actual origin story of the "treacherous Indian." In parallel with Blanton's study, I argue that the scarcity of environmental references in the early Spanish chronicles reflects the Europeans' unfamiliarity with their new surroundings and not the absence or irrelevance of such factors. My hypothesis is that the 1494-1496 famine on Hispaniola may have been similar to the Jamestown situation described by Blanton; that a climatic extreme event such as a prolonged phase of drought may have depleted the Arawak food resources in such a way that they were unable to feed the additional 1,500 men Columbus brought with him on his second voyage (Fernandez de Oviedo y Váldez 1851 (1535), II, VIII, 35). Considering the cultural and linguistic barriers, such a deviation from the climatic norm would have been difficult for the Arawak to communicate to the European newcomers. Lacking any longer-term experience with the tropical climate and environment of Hispaniola, the Spanish thus turned to the social sphere in search of an explanation. Following established patterns of explanation for famine and starvation (such as blaming the "corn Jew" mentioned above), they interpreted the unavailability of indigenous foodstuffs as a sly strategy by this newly discovered group of "heathens" to expel them from the island. In the argumentation of the Spanish chroniclers, framing the absence of foodstuffs as a revenge coup made particular sense in view of the earlier violence of the colonists towards the indigenous population.

Las Casas writes about the perceived indigenous unwillingness to provide the Spaniards with food that

> [...] many of them [the Arawaks] decided to assist them [the Spaniards] with a trick or a warning, so that they would die or leave the island [...]. The warning was this (even though it had the contrary effect of what they expected), the Indians neither sowed nor did they work their Conucos,[7] so that no harvest would be obtained on the island [...]. (Casas et al. 1875 (1575), II, CVI, 106)

D'Anghiera in his *De Orbe Novo Decades* (Decades of the New World), on the other hand, writes:

> [Columbus] was informed that the natives suffered from such a severe famine that more than 50,000 men had already perished, and that people continued to die daily as cattle in time of a pest. This calamity was the consequence of their own folly; for when they saw that the Spaniards wished to settle in their island, they thought they might expel them by creating a scarcity of food. They therefore decided not only to plant no more crops, but also to destroy and tear up all the various kinds of cereals used for bread which had already been sown [...] (Parry and Keith 1984, 209).

D'Anghiera starts with the indigenous famine and only in a second step assigns it to the Arawak "strategy" of uprooting the already planted crops to starve out the Spaniards. A little further on in his

7 Conucos are raised plots or mounds that were planted with food crops (Sauer 1966, 51).

account, he describes the Spanish introduction of tribute payments upon the Arawak but that the famine prevented them from achieving such payments and that they begged Columbus to "have pity on their misery and to exempt them till such time as the island might recover its former prosperity" (Parry and Keith 1984, 210). In the first part of the account, the human agency as a cause for the famine seems to be clear, though it almost comes as an afterthought. The following paragraphs where the Arawak ask for a delay of tribute payments does not repeat that connection to "their own folly." So, is it possible to assume that the trope of destroying their own crops may be a European substitute for an otherwise unexplainable food scarcity?

Fernandez de Oviedo's *Historia General*, in particular, provides clues that may support this hypothesis. Similar to what Blanton observes for the historical records in the case of Jamestown, neither Fernandez de Oviedo nor the other chroniclers make direct remarks about local weather conditions that they connect to the famine. Again, it's important to underline that despite the search for culprits in the social realm, some of the natural causality of climatic extreme events was well understood in medieval and early modern Europe. Grape harvest dates, high water levels in rivers, storms, and extreme cold or heat were regularly noted in (church) chronicles. In other words, the practice of observing local weather conditions was well-established (Jankovic 2000; Mauelshagen 2018). The scarcity of references to weather/environment is therefore conspicuous and would rather support the claim that it does not signify absence of phenomena but absence of familiarity with phenomena.

But back to Oviedo. He echoes las Casas and d'Anghiera in saying the Arawak had invented a "malicious ploy" (*un mal ardid*) after they had realized that the Spaniards were planning on settling for good on the island.

> Because of this, more than half of the Spaniards died, and of the Indians so many died that they could not be counted. And this occurred in such a way that it could not be prevented or understood *because this land was so new for the Christians, they could not car-*

> *ry out the work they were accustomed to nor did they understand it.* And it occurred thus: All Indians of this province agreed on not sowing anything at the time when they should have done it; and as they did not have maize they ate yuca, which are the two kinds of bread and the main means of subsistence that exist in this country. The Christians ate their own foodstuffs and when those were finished, they sought to help themselves to the crops of the earth which the Indians cultivated, but they didn't have any, neither for themselves nor for [the Spaniards]. In this way, many men died of hunger in this city of the Christians. (Fernandez de Oviedo y Váldez, 1851 (1535), II, XIII, 49, emphasis added)

Oviedo continued that the Fort of Santo Tomás had experienced the same fate, that half of its Spanish population had died of hunger and that the Arawak had been even more severely affected by the famine. "In this way, the Indians carried out their malicious plan of expelling the Christians from the Island for lack of provisions […]." (Ibid.) Even though such historic mortality figures have to be treated with caution, Oviedo's account coincides quite well with the death toll Dennis Blanton reconstructs in his Jamestown study, he speaks of a mortality rate of about 60 percent (Blanton 2000, 78).

Of course, it could be entirely correct to take las Casas, d'Anghiera and Oviedo by their word and interpret the events of 1494-1496 as a war strategy of the Arawak, in which they were prepared to accept the mass-death of their own people. The research currently dealing with the famine assumes a mixture of such a war strategy combined with European diseases and overwork as a reason for the high mortality rates. For example, George Raudzens in a 1996 article that compares the European invasions of Hispaniola and Virginia claims that "passive resistance led them [the Arawaks] to destroy their own food so that the Spanish would also starve" (Raudzens 1996, 339). In light of the results of Blanton's study and of what we know about early modern perceptions of famines and extreme events, I am not convinced by this at-face-value acceptance of primary accounts. I find the idea that a society would commit mass-suicide by destroying its own food sources – even under the shocking circumstances of Spanish violence and pathogens – extremely implausible. If we were to believe in the starving-out-account, should we not trust that in such a scenario, people who were intimately familiar with the environment and topography of their island as the Arawak would have been as smart as creating a secret stash of foodstuffs in order to bring the war strategy to fruition and secure the survival of their own community?

To clarify, I do not argue for climatic factors as a single cause for the 1494 famine, in particular in light of the convincing evidence regarding European diseases and violent coercion as factors that would disrupt agricultural activity and may thus already create an impasse in food provision. But I would like to introduce climatic factors into the debate as one, possibly as decisive a factor as those others that should be considered. Even if we have to get to climatic factors via several detours as the historical records do not speak about what we would call climatic phenomena explicitly. With his statement about the land being so "new" to the colonists, Oviedo provides a contemporary explanation for the difficulty of the Spaniards to read their unfamiliar environment properly. The missing maize and the shift to yuca (a root crop also known as cassava or manioc) could very well be related to climatic factors such as extreme drought. Furthermore, the fact that Oviedo states that the indigenous population did not have crops for themselves nor for the Spaniards could be an indication that this was precisely *not* a strategy but that possibly a larger-scale environmental phenomenon was contributing to the situation. This latter assumption is substantiated by Oviedo's account of Santo Tomás, about 100 km further southeast of la Isabela, which experienced the same fate.

From my current point of view there are two scenarios which may provide an explanation for the 1494-1496 famine. Scenario A: Climatic factors did not play a role; the famine was caused by the mass-death of the Arawak due to European diseases and the consequent situation that not enough people were available to plant maize and yuca. A point that remains somewhat implausible in this scenario is, why the Spaniards should not have managed to nourish themselves under normal climatic circumstances in an environment that had been described as abundant in flora and fauna (particularly fish) by contemporaries (Navarrete 1825, 209).

Scenario B: Climatic factors *did* play a role. Even though we do not have verbal descriptions of conditions that could have affected human food production (at least not in the kind of terminology that we might expect from a present-day point of view), we know from the early chronicles that in 1494 as well as 1495 Hispaniola was hit by a hurricane.

> In the month of June of this same year [1494] occurred a frightful tempest; whirlwinds reaching to the skies uprooted the largest trees that were swept within their vortex. [...] It is said that in that year the sea penetrated more deeply than usual into the earth, and that it rose more than a cubit. (Parry and Keith 1984, 211)

wrote d'Anghiera about the 1494 hurricane.[8] The additional information he gives about the flood depth caused by the hurricane is interesting with regard to assessing its strength. Since the hurricane seasons of 2017 and 2019 have proven exceptionally destructive for the islands of the Caribbean, I do not have to argue for the fact that what we perceive as devastating storms today (even minus the increased strength through climate change), would have been devastating for historically less developed societies that depended entirely on agricultural crops for their subsistence back then. Particularly a maize harvest would have been easily razed by a hurricane.

Climatologically, active hurricane seasons and an increase in sea surface temperatures in the Caribbean are associated with La Niña conditions, the cold phase (cooling sea surface temperatures in the Pacific off the coast of Peru) of the climatic phenomenon known as the El Niño Southern Oscillation (ENSO). If this is coupled with a southerly position of a second important climatic system known as the Inter-Tropical Convergence Zone, or ITCZ, hurricanes are more

---

8 Both hurricanes are accepted by Millás (Millás and Pardue 1968, 7). On the treatment of hurricanes in historical records see Rohland 2019 (chapter 1).

likely to take more southerly courses and to hit the Caribbean archipelago, rather than entering the Gulf of Mexico or affecting the east coast of the U.S. (Burn et al. 2016; Grove and Adamson 2018; Malaizé et al. 2011). Clues from a historical reconstruction of such ENSO data (Emile-Geay et al. 2013) point to a multi-year la Niña-phase between 1492 and 1495.

Oviedo, though he did not write about weather phenomena in a causal relation with the famine, continued his account of 1494 by saying that the "exhaustion and fatigues" of the Spaniards were ongoing and that, to top things off, "winds were blowing from the north (which in Castilla are called çierço) and which make this island sick." As a result, "not only Christians died, but also the natural Indians." (Fernandez de Oviedo y Váldez, 1851 (1535), II, XIII, 51) The references to "fatigues," "sickness," and north winds are very inconclusive and hard to place in a causal relationship. Nevertheless, they are significant, since the effects seem to hit Spaniards and Arawak alike and no references are made anymore to the plan of the indigenous population to oust the Spaniards. What is more, similar wording reappears in the colonial correspondence of the Santo Dominguan *Cabildo* of the sixteenth century, indicating environmental stress on the island (AGI, *Gobierno*, Leg. 73, see for example years 1550, 1555, 1557, 1560, 1573, 1576).

So, apart from the – so far – admittedly inconclusive evidence for a "climatic factor hypothesis" from the human archives that my examples share with Blanton's, could the "natural archives," that is, paleoclimatic proxy-records,[9] provide more information about envi-

9 Climatic conditions (temperature and precipitation averages) of the past can be reconstructed by way of using either written historical documents (what climate historians and historical climatologists call "human archives") and/or data reconstructed from natural sources such as ice cores, speleothems, corals, lake sediments etc. (so called proxy records which belong to the "natural archives"). Both kinds of records require careful and critical scrutiny and a complex reconstruction process in order to arrive at viable numerical data. For more in-depth information on this operation see Mauelshagen 2010 and White, Pfister and Mauelshagen 2018.

ronmental conditions at the time of the 1494-1496 famine? Before we look into possible answers to this question, first a short orientation as to the climatological "epoch" in which our Hispaniolan famine example is set. Over the last decade, it has become common for climate and early modern historians to speak about the Little Ice Age (LIA hereafter), an era of decreased air temperature of the northern hemisphere by c. 0.6 to 0.8 degrees Celsius that some climatologists set to start in 1400 and to last until 1800 (Burn and Palmer 2014).[10] It is misleading, however, to think of the LIA as a period of uniformly colder conditions, since local effects varied greatly. Reduced solar irradiation and an uptick in global volcanic activity have been suggested as causes for the LIA. While the socio-environmental cooling effects of the beginning of the LIA is well-documented for northern Europe (Alberola Roma 2014; Camenisch 2015; Campbell 2016; Pfister and Brázdil 1999, 2006; Pribyl 2017), evidence of equally significant effects of the LIA on the tropics has started to come together more recently (Lane et al. 2011). Due to the relative dearth of documentary evidence from the early LIA period in the American tropics (as evidenced in my example above) the data for this region so far overwhelmingly stem from the natural archives.

Three recent papers on climatic conditions in the Caribbean during the LIA (Burn and Palmer 2014, 2015; Lane et al. 2011) converge in interesting ways in their findings. All three state that during the LIA, conditions in the (Circum-)Caribbean turned significantly dryer compared to earlier periods of observation. Lane et al. state that these drought conditions were identified for geographically distinct regions such as the Yucatan Peninsula, Panama, northern South America, Puerto Rico and along the southern slope of the Dominican Republic's Cordillera Central, where they took their sedimentary sample (Lane et al. 2011, 467). This underlines the fact that

10 Other datings are from 1257-1850, or 1300-1850, or 1550-1850 and there is no real agreement among climatologists. Currently the concept has become so embattled that some scholars would abolish it altogether (Mauelshagen 2010).

these changing climatic conditions of the LIA not only affected isolated areas but were of a synoptic-scale extension. Lane et al.'s evidence from northern South America indicate that the LIA might have been the driest period of the last 10'000 years in the Circum-Caribbean (Lane et al. 2011, 462).

These indications from recent paleoclimate studies with lake sediment samples from Hispaniola and nearby Jamaica are highly significant with regard to our question of the influence of climatic factors and support my hypothesis to a certain extent. Yet, the temporal resolution of lake sediment cores – i.e. the possibility to assign soil layers that indicate drought to specific years – is rather rough compared to a proxy such as tree rings, which have an annual resolution in the temperate latitudes. However, tree rings are not as readily available in tropical regions since only few tropical tree varieties produce visible rings due to the lack of strong seasonal variability. In other words, more fine-grained analyses of climatic conditions at the time of Columbus' arrival on the island have yet to be made. Or in Lane et al.'s conclusive sentence: "the potential impacts of LIA aridity on human society warrant further attention" (Lane et al. 2011, 469).

So, in light of the evidence from the natural archives I will close my argument for scenario B and climatic factors with the tentative assumption that the 1494-1496 famine on Hispaniola was caused by the combined factors of a prolonged drought, repeated damages to food crops from hurricanes, as well as by the indigenous mortality rates caused by European epidemics and by European violence mentioned in scenario A above.

After this somewhat meandering walk through the Spanish first/early contact situation on Hispaniola and climatic evidence from paleoclimate studies, where does this leave us with regard to practices of comparing and entanglement? How did comparison play a role in these early years of Spanish presence in an unfamiliar environment and climate? Historically, practices of comparing are most easily to be discovered in written sources where two units (or *com-*

*parata*) are compared with regard to a third, the *tertium comparationis*, such as Columbus' comparison of Hispaniola's landscape and nature with Castile mentioned above. It is rather more difficult to account for practices of comparing that we have to infer or historically reconstruct because they did not form part of a discourse or were not made explicit in writing. I would suggest that the 1494-1496 famine on Hispaniola is such a case of a non-discursive comparative practice and at the same time a situation of incomparability. I arrive at the latter, incomparability, not so much by the appraisal of the contemporaries themselves but rather by inference through historical analysis. Let me explain. At the beginning of the chapter we've followed Christopher Columbus across the Atlantic and along his comparison of tropical Ayiti/Hispaniola with Castile and Cordoba. The gravity of this environmental comparison, its impulse for concrete action, and in particular its far-reaching material consequences have been captured by Crosby's concept of the *Columbian Exchange*. Columbus' comparison(s) can be termed "discursive" since they appear in a particular genre – a logbook – that was meant to be read by a public audience (most notably the king and queen of Castile). In addition, Columbus' account stands in the tradition of the ancient Greek *periploi* and Greek cosmographical and geographical knowledge early modern explorers were referencing explain the (world-)knowledge of their own time (Matei-Chesnoiu 2015; Schulz 2016).

By analogy with Blanton's study of Jamestown which has the advantage of paleoclimatic evidence to underline its claim, I have set up the hypothesis that the Spanish in Hispaniola had been even more clearly in a situation of unfamiliarity with the unknown (natural and social) environment of the New World than the English a hundred years later. They could at least refer back to the Spanish experience and their accounts of first contact. For the Spaniards in 1492, unfamiliarity with the new environment literally meant incomparability of phenomena on the experiential level and hence a necessity to draw on the "home-grown" patterns of social and environmental knowledge from Spain and ancient Greece. This environmental unfamiliarity, and hence, the absence of a local frame of reference is briefly mentioned by Fernandez de Oviedo in his account of the famine. This is the implicit reason, given by contemporaries themselves, for the incomparability of phenomena. This incomparability of the environmental realm and the consequent search for causality in the social sphere led to the projection of the conspiracy theory of the treacherous, food-hiding Indian that is referenced by the English on the Chesapeake Bay a century later. From both Columbus' report as well as the later Spanish chroniclers' accounts it emerges, then, that discursive as well as non-discursive practices of comparing can be constitutive for entangled histories, in particular with regard to environmental factors. The early inter-American and transatlantic entanglement is underlined by the fact that Spanish conquest reports were used for comparison by the English and that, with the arrival of the English on the Chesapeake Bay, the conspiracy theory spread to this new region and was presented to a new audience.

Environmental factors of entanglement have appeared in different guises throughout this chapter and have shaped unequal relationships of power on Hispaniola and later also on what contemporaries called *tierra firme* (the continent) from the get-go.

At the beginning of this chapter, I have mentioned the dearth of silver in Europe as a driving factor for the Spanish to seek this resource elsewhere and arrive at the shores of Ayiti in the first place; I briefly touched on the well-trodden soil of the Columbian Exchange and European pathogens as a factor in the unequal playing field between Spaniards and Arawaks in the Caribbean (and later other indigenous peoples of the continent); with the examples of Jamestown and Hispaniola we've seen the importance of climatic factors (and the knowledge of such factors) for the English and Spanish in trying to get a foothold in this newly discovered world and in forging their relationships with the indigenous population; and again a more familiar aspect of environmental entanglement is that of the Spanish coercion of Arawak labor in order to extract gold from Hispaniolan mines, that is, the entanglement of economic strife, natural resources, colonial power, and energy – the muscle-power of forced indigenous labor.

On the interpretive level, this chapter has shown the force of comparison in a colonial first contact situation set in an unfamiliar – and, at the time, incomparable – environment. The reconstruction of a non-discursive comparative practice in this context has shown how practices of comparing can be constitutive for processes of entanglement. On an epistemic level, the inclusion of environmental factors into the concept of Entangled history also underlines the need for strongly interdisciplinary approaches. Dennis Blanton, an archaeologist, has used paleoclimatic data, historical records and archaeological sources to arrive at his conclusions. I am relying on research from the same disciplines that cross the divide between the natural sciences and the humanities for my analysis of the famine on Hispaniola. In other words, consistently integrating the environment into Entangled history also means doing historical research with a new openness to and willingness to collaborate with other disciplines.

The following chapter starts out in the eighteenth century and the by-then fixed notion that Africans were "naturally" suited to be enslaved and to perform slave labor in the tropics due to their tropical origins. The chapter dissects this idea by following its genealogy through history and employing the double perspective of environment-in-entanglement and practices of comparing. This transports the narrative back to Columbus' first contact with the Arawak, unfolding a new layer of complexity in the notion of "unfamiliar environments" and peoples while showing how environmental factors are entangled with images of indigenous and African bodies in the formation of the concept of "race."

## 3. Extracting: Comparing European and African Bodies in Tropical Climates

> By some, it has been with considerable ingenuity argued, that the change of colour is merely a consequence of the heat of climate, exposure to the sun, and inattention to cleanliness. […] Slavery is peculiarly congenial, and seems even to be natural to the inhabitants of warm climates. […] In tropical regions, the necessaries of life are so easily procured, frequently springing spontaneously, and protection from the inclemencies of heaven are so little required, and so easily attained, that the energies of the human mind being never excited, are suffered to remain in eternal slumber. Of this situation, sloth is a natural, almost necessary consequence; and indolence being the parent of weakness, submission to injustice and violence, without murmur, reflection, or resentment, generally takes place. (Renny 1807, 160-161)

Even being an abolitionist and publishing these words right around the time of the abolition of the African slave trade throughout the British Empire, Jamaican historian Joseph Renny was repeating some of the most prevalent European *topoi* about Africans, the presumed (environmentally caused) nature of their skin color, their "natural suitability" for forced labor due to their tropical origins, and the morally debasing qualities of the tropics on the human character in general. At the end of the eighteenth and the turn to the nineteenth century, these tropes, in particular in the French and British Caribbean had gained specific inflections, had solidified in some respects and lost some explanatory power in others as we will see throughout this chapter.

After following environmental factors from Columbus' arrival on Hispaniola, we now arrive at the question of how environmental factors played a role in European capitalist exploitation of the Caribbean island soils and of human (forced) labor. That is, this chapter will explore, not so much the place of the plantation and of African slavery in the entangled history(ies) of the Caribbean and the Atlantic – many others have done this more eloquently and eruditely (Blackburn 2010; Eltis 2000; Hanger 1993; Klein and Vinson 2007; Schwartz 2004). Rather, I want to trace the *justification* for this extractivist system through the lens of environmental entanglements and practices of comparing. In the British, the French, and the Spanish (Circum-)Caribbean, the enslavement of African peoples and their violent exploitation in Caribbean sugar plantations was justified by some variant of the argument we saw Renny make above, that they were better adapted to the hot climate of the islands, since they, too, came from tropical regions.

While the previous chapters focused more strongly on colonial accounts of lived (socio-)environmental experience such as famines and hurricanes and their perceived causes, this chapter will move somewhat more into the territory of the social construction of environment and "climate," in particular. We will keep one foot in the material world, however, since the socially constructed climate of the tropics is closely related to the historical (European) experience and description of these phenomena. It is in fact exactly this interface between the "material" and the constructed climate and the moral coding, which Europeans such as Renny assigned to the tropics, that made this argument powerful throughout Spanish, French, and British colonial history. So powerful, in fact, that such climate-determinism remained alive and in use until well into the 20$^{th}$ century and the postcolonial period. I would therefore argue that this "pre-adaptedness-of-African-bodies-to-tropical-climates" trope is one of the most important (and vicious) drivers in the entangled histories of the Caribbean and a strong example of the importance of considering environmental factors in entanglement/entangled history. In order to trace the European reasoning behind this *topos*, we will have to follow its constituent parts as far back through history as we can in order to contextualize them and see them shift their meaning though time. I will therefore rather use Renny as a springboard which will catapult us back to sixteenth-century Europe and the Spanish Caribbean in order to see how slavery in general, and slavery in the Americas in particular, was justified at this early stage. I will then move forward again on the timeline of this trope, back to the end of the eighteenth century. Several questions need to be clarified along the way, however, such as how the environment or climate could even be conceived of as having an effect on the body and/or character and on skin color in particular. How did arguments that connect environment and skin color then lead to the argument of enslavement of certain peoples? How were "tropical climate" and adaptation – the actual historical term used in the eighteenth century was *acclimatization* – understood? A cursory exploration of this conceptual history follows below, and, as may be evident, will also bring us to the rise and evolution of the idea of "race."

Similar to chapter 2, *Arriving*, the present chapter with its focus on African slavery in the Caribbean covers a lot of familiar historical ground. My case study is not the first to point out that "climate" was used as an argument for slavery in the Americas (Cañizares Esguerra 2009a; Newman 2018; Schiebinger 2017; Seth 2014, 2018). In this chapter, mainly based on the excellent secondary literature dealing with environmental influences on white, Indian, and black bodies in early colonial New Spain, the British and French (Circum-)Caribbean, I will probe deeper into the conceptual layers mentioned above while, again, showing how practices of comparing are fundamental or even generators for entangled history(ies).

## Human Bodies and the Environment in Early Modern European Thinking

Let's start with the idea of the body then, and the question how the environment could influence skin color and could influence the body in such a way that it could be considered "pre-adapted" to a specific climate – and work form. And, in fact, let's start this inquiry in Europe in order to see how these issues were discussed among the learned elite around the end of the fifteenth century and the time of Columbus' journey to the New World.

The Early modern understanding of the human body and the maintenance of its health revolved around the concept of "complexion" (Groebner 2004). It formed the center of humoral pathology which had been developed from the writings collected in the *Corpus Hippocraticum* in the fourth century BCE and which had been integrated into Galenic medical knowledge during the second century CE. These ancient traditions had been re-appropriated and reworked in Europe, including Arabian texts (Avicenna and Averroes), during the eleventh and twelfth century (Rütten 2012, 61; Siraisi 1990). In its late medieval and early modern understanding, complexion did not merely refer to a person's face or their skin, it included their whole appearance, their behavior, moral condition, and aptitude. Each person had their individual complexion, which was governed by a specific balance of the four humors, the basic building blocks of human health: blood, phlegm, black bile and yellow bile. Each of these was associated with qualities such as heat or cold, dryness or moisture and, through these qualities, was naturally linked to the four elements, which formed the basis of all substance. Furthermore, each humor, together with its quality and element was related to a season (Earle 2012, 26).

In addition, the heaven (stars and planets) could have a significant influence on the complexion since the elemental qualities of the complexion were mirrored in the different planets. That is, Mars was thought to be hot and dry, Venus to be cold and wet. Astrological constellations with their qualities were thought to be causally related to a person and their organs' complexion(s) (Groebner 2004, 365-368). Complexion was simultaneously fixed in the sense that each person had their unique complexion, and malleable, as it could change with "age, emotions, with the impact of disease and medication and even with changes of the weather" (ibid., 369). Historian of colonial Latin America, Rebecca Earle, stresses the central role that food played as a mediator of a healthy complexion, in particular in the early modern Spanish discourse about nature and living conditions for Spaniards in the New World (Earle 2012, 28). This brief outline already hints at how deeply humans and their physique were thought to be entangled with the environment, which included the planets.

Bringing together the so far rather internal qualities of the Galenic understanding of complexion with the external aspect of skin color, medieval historian Valentin Groebner quotes bodily descriptions of female slaves of mixed geographical backgrounds that were bought and sold in Florence at the end of the fourteenth century. These medieval Florentine slave registers and notary records provided various hues of skin color, including olive-colored, brown, red, yellow, white, black, and even "greenish" along with various other bodily features such as moles, scars or tattoos. Often, such assignment of color remained inconclusive since it was not clear whether it referred to the skin, its marks, or to hair (Groebner 2004, 374-375). According to Groebner, "very few of the inhabitants of Renaissance Europe seem to have considered themselves to be white in any form [...]. On the contrary, European theories of climate and complexion handed down from the classics reserved a number of rather unflattering terms for the fair-haired and fair-skinned people of the north" (ibid., 377). Aristotle, Pliny, and Vitruvius all agreed on the influence of the environment on the human body. According to them, cold northern regions rendered their inhabitants hardy, but because there was not enough heat that could make moisture evaporate, this moisture settled on northerner's minds and made them slow and dull-witted (ibid., 378).

This ancient "Hippocratic environmentalism" and "Galenic humoralism" (Cagle 2018, 142), was also at the core of how early modern Europeans thought about themselves as "nations" (i.e. Spaniards, French or English) and which peoples belonged to them and which did not (Feros 2017, 109-152). It formed the basis of influential renaissance writers' thinking such as the French jurist and political philosopher Jean Bodin in his *Methodus ad facilem historiarum cogitionem* (Method for the Easy Comprehension of History) (Bodin 1566). In his chapter on the "Correct evaluation of histories," he suggests that cold and phlegmatic people were living in the north and that skin colors varied depending on geographical region. Leuko-Ethiopians, for example, lived in different regions and "under the tropics are unusually black; under the pole, for the opposite reason, they are tawny in color [...]" (Bodin and Reynolds 1945, 89). In the course of this account of different peoples and latitudes, Bodin lists further environmentally induced skin tones that range from white through yellow, green and black and are noted without apparent value judgement (Bodin 1945, 89). Groebner concludes that the early modern European idea of complexion, much like its medieval predecessor, was a relational category that did not stand for itself but came in "neatly preorganized juxtapositions." The latter, however, hardened in the course of colonial expansion and the consequent necessity for creating new political boundaries (Groebner 2004, 383).

So, according to Groebner's account and Earle's summary of humoral pathological knowledge in early modern Spanish learning, to sixteenth-century Europeans, the human body and constitution (including skin color) were governed on the macro-scale by the geographical region they lived in and the latter's respective astrological constellations. On the micro-scale, individual habits, the weather, and even food could alter complexion.

It is important to briefly note at this point that until the turn of the nineteenth century, "climate" in the context of what has been said so far did not mean "average weather over a certain space of time" involving measures of precipitation and temperature as we understand it today. The notion of a "climate theory," which is often projected into sixteenth or seventeenth century (or even earlier) historical agents by present-day historians, is a misconception. Our modern understanding of "climate" only starts emerging at the beginning of the nineteenth century as the result of a long process of scientific evolution. "Climate" (from Greek *klima*) was a geographical demarcation meaning "inclination," referring to the inclination of the sun's rays, which varies with latitude. In Ptolemaic world maps and globes, *klimata* demarcated half-hour differences of sunshine on the longest day of the year. It was a geographic measure to locate places on a map and not a term related to meteorology. "Speaking of the 'climate' of a place was equivalent to giving its latitudinal coordinates on the globe rather than explaining heat or cold, rainfall or humidity" (Mauelshagen 2018, 566). Meteorological "zones" – as in the "torrid", the "temperate" and the "frigid zone" – were a different concept, mentioned in Aristotle's *Meteorology*, that existed alongside and independent of the *klimata*. Since the nineteenth century, the ancient geographic concept of *klimata* has been anachronistically confused or equalized with Aristotle's meteorological zones. However, in Renaissance Europe there existed a practice of connecting the seven climates of the "inhabited world" to the seven (known) planets. In this way, the seven Ptolemaian *klimata* became related to the humors and hence to the human body and its complexion. While the mathematically accurate half hour climates remained a common feature on maps into the eighteenth century, the notion of the seven inhabited climates lost traction with the European expansion and experience of indigenous peoples in previously unknown places around the globe (ibid., 570).

So, to return to the connection of skin color and environments, if the connection between climates and properties of heat, cold or moisture were made, this meant, as in Mauelshangen's quote above, that such heat, cold or moisture were present in this latitude or geographical region. And as Bodin's assessment of the Leuko-Ethiopians, who had different skin colors according to the latitude they were located in, shows, the hues of human skin were thought to be mutable as well and not a fixed, innate, biological property. Which brings us to the concept of "race." At the turn of the seventeenth century, the term was not in any way fixed on such physical appearances yet. Consulting a trilingual (Spanish, French, Italian) dictionary published in 1609, we find the Castilian "raça" translated in terms of "lineage" and "generation" (Girolamo 1609), showing the contemporary concern with genealogy in order to establish that one was Spanish and a Christian, in particular for Jewish or Muslim converts (Feros 2017; Cañizares Esguerra 2009a). At this early stage, and in the European context, the term "race" did therefore not have the biogenetic implications that it has today (Aubert 2004; Carrera 2003; Chaplin 2002; Newman 2018; Schiebinger 2017).

With regard to environmental factors in entanglement, this short overview has shown how, almost as a sort of default-setting, early modern conceptions of the body and "complexion" deeply connected humans with their respective environments. With its roots in Greek antiquity and the later addition of Arabian medical knowledge and astrology, the longevity of this understanding of how humans were entangled with the environment becomes evident. So far, the descriptions of geographical regions, complexions and skin colors have sounded rather matter of fact and dispassionate, as stated above: without value judgement. How, then, did the perception of black color as a negative quality that marked people as potentially "enslaveable" enter the picture? Bodin gives a brief hint that, in fact, marks a general and important pattern in European intellectual discourse for the justification of enslaving Africans. In an earlier paragraph than the one on the Leuko-Ethiopians quoted above, Bodin talks about the conditions of the tropics, the burning heat, that there were "no woods, few rivers and perpetual flatness of the sands." To this he adds that, not only the Ethiopians[11] (who lived under the tropics) had black skin but also the Indians (of India). "I can hardly be persuaded that men are made black from the curse of Chus, as a certain learned man reports" (Bodin 1945, 87). With this remark, Bodin referred to the biblical story of the son of Noah (also called Cham or Ham), which was the other line of argument for how black skin color came about, and also for the enslavement of Africans, as we will see in a moment.

In his chapter on Complexion, Groebner quotes mostly continental European sources and – judging from his secondary literature – rather the Anglo- and French early modern perspective on things, while the Spanish and Spanish New World experience is missing from his account. For our questions on how environmental factors

---

11 *Ethiopia(n)* is the Greek translation of Hebrew *Kush(ite)*, both terms etymologically mean "burnt face," i.e. dark skinned. The term *Ethiopia(n)* moved from Greek into Latin and other European languages, and outside the biblical context came to mean "black Africa(n)." See Goldenberg 2017, 7-8.

could be seen to influence skin color and how this nexus could become an argument for slavery, the Spanish colonial perspective is crucial, however. Quoting Ann-Laura Stoler, historian Jorge Cañizares Esguerra has argued that the colonial peripheries were "laboratories of modernity," where the question of "race," in particular, came to be discussed with an urgency during the mid-sixteenth and early seventeenth century that had no match in Europe at the time (Cañizares Esguerra 1999, 68). And despite the fact that the French jurist Jean Bodin was doubtful whether the Curse of Ham had anything to do with black skin color, this biblical story had apparently served as a justification for the subordination of peasants and Jews, as well as for the enslavement of Africans since antiquity.

Cañizares Esguerra in a 2009 article subtitled "The Early Modern Body in the Tropics" unfurls another layer of complexity in the nexus of the environment, the body and the question of enslavement (Cañizares Esguerra 2009a). Cañizares Esguerra starts out by explaining how the connection between heresy and permanent demonic transformations of the body were imagined in early modern Spain. Heresy did not only taint the body and being of the heretic him or herself, it affected his or her direct bloodline into the fourth generation (Cañizares Esguerra 2009a, 315). Heresy was thus an inheritable, physical condition that needed to be disproven by a "clean" bloodline (*limpieza de sangre*), which, through the meaning of "lineage," connects back to the definition of "raça," quoted above. In early modern Spain, *conversos* and *moriscos* (converted Jews or Muslims and their descendants) were considered at risk of falling back into these "enemy faiths" and were therefore particularly suspicious. The Inquisition devised a rigorous system of questioning such individuals based on genealogical records, which was however, according to Cañizares Esguerra, easy to manipulate. Ultimately, such questionings (*probanzas*) rather became a way for *conversos* and *moriscos* to delete the memories of their non-Christian backgrounds rather than a racialized stigmatization of their persons (ibid., 318).

Yet, the Christian idea of tainting a bloodline for generations through heresy, sin or moral wrongdoing also lies at the heart of the story of the Curse of Ham (Genesis 9: 18-25) mentioned above. According to Cañizares Esguerra, this narrative "did its dirty ideological work" in the Americas, along with another curse story (Jacob cursing Issachar), which was used as a justification for indigenous slavery (Cañizares Esguerra 2009a, 316). With regard to the Curse of Ham, we have seen that Bodin doubted Noah's curse as the origin of black skin – not only in "Ethiopians" but also in Indians (of India). This means, however, that such a line of reasoning existed at the time of Bodin's writing his *Methodus* in the mid-sixteenth century. At the same time, this curse was also considered to be the origin story for slavery, in such a way that the two aspects became conflated and emerged as the biblical reference in support of the enslavement of dark-skinned, and African people in particular.

In several publications, Near Eastern and Judaic Studies scholar David Goldenberg retraced and untangled the combination of both, the storyline of slavery and the one of the origins of black skin color (Goldenberg 2003, 2017). He found that they are, in fact two separate biblical stories, one of rabbinic origin in which Noah's son Ham was rendered black after committing a sin on the Ark, and one of Christian origin (the one in Genesis 9) in which Noa's son Ham commits a sin and Noah curses Ham's son Canaan and his descendants to slavery (Goldenberg 2017, 25-27). These two stories underwent a complex morphological process in the ancient Near East. Goldenberg was able to trace the connection between skin color and enslavement to Muslim traditions and in particular to the time of Muslim conquests in Africa during the 7$^{th}$ century. The increase in enslavement of Africans during this time influenced the conflation of black skin color and servitude not only in real life but also in the way the biblical story was understood: "The dual form of the Curse of Ham, in which black skin is part of the curse, was a direct result of the increasing importation of black slaves to Arab lands, and the consequent degradation of their status. This was an important development in the Curse of Ham saga, for the dual curse more profoundly tied blackness to servitude." It is at this point that black skin color in the perception of lighter-skinned North Africans and Europeans historically evolved into an intentional marker of servitude (ibid., 199-200). This conflated version of the Curse of Ham made its way from the East to the Iberian Peninsula via the Muslim conquest and its cultural influences, and from there, as we will see in a moment, to the Caribbean from the sixteenth century onwards.

So, from the above it has become clear how in the Judeo-Christian and Muslim religious traditions the idea of sin as an inheritable physical property, black skin color as a curse and punishment, and slavery as a curse and punishment have become linked. Why, however, should black skin color be inherently negatively stigmatized? Anthropologically speaking, skin color etiologies seem to be a universal phenomenon. Societies with a more or less uniform skin color who came in contact with peoples of a markedly different color would develop an etiology that would explain how the difference had come about. Such skin-color etiologies exist in post-European-contact Native American societies, but also in dark-skinned societies, explaining the existence of lighter-skinned individuals (ibid., 28). For our question above, the ancient Greek case is – maybe unsurprisingly – informative again. When ancient Greek explorers discovered the existence of dark-skinned African peoples, they developed two lines of argument to account for their skin color. The first one we've already encountered, even if mediated through early modern European texts, namely, that because these peoples lived to the south of the Greeks, they were burnt dark by the heat of the sun. Those to the north were white because of the lack of sunlight, and, remembering the Greek ethno-geographical knowledge transmitted by Bodin, they were also sluggish and a bit dumb because of the excess moisture in the northern air. The Greeks, from their own point of view, were just the right color and complexion.

The second line of argument was a mythological one. It held that Phaeton, the son of sun god Helios, had brought the sun chariot too close to the earth and in the course had burnt the peoples of Ethiopia (ibid., 29). In other words, by way of ancient Greek ethno-geographical knowledge that was accessible to European explorers of the fifteenth and following centuries, the environmental line of the argument for black skin color remained in the explanatory repertoire of Europeans. The Greek mythology, on the other hand, was replaced by the Judeo-Christian-Muslim mythology as it had evolved in the Near East.

It is important to note that the environmental argument was by no means a neutral one. The "just right" conditions were always positively biased towards the eye of the beholder, which was often representative of an Empire. Claiming "Goldilocks conditions" for one's own people was (and is), apparently, a human universal as much as skin color etiologies. Greeks, Romans, Chinese, Italians, Spanish, French, English and Germans claimed these conditions for themselves at various times through history (ibid., 29; Groebner 2004, 379).

## Spanish, Indian, and African Bodies in the American Tropics

Even though the narrative of the Curse of Ham as outlined by Goldenberg and Cañizares Esguerra suggests that a connection between black skin and servitude had been made in the Judeo-Christian-Muslim context of the Near East and that the narrative or content of this biblical curse story had spread throughout the Iberian Peninsula by the end of the fifteenth century, the question remains, how pervasive and potent it actually was, in particular in the context of the early Portuguese expansion along the African West Coast. Looking at this history of expansion, which immediately preceded Columbus' trying to reach "India" by sailing west, and which laid the foundation for the later African slave trade, the emerging picture is more complex than the curse story and its implied power differential might suggest.

In a first instance, the environment in the form of Aristotle's meteorological zones – in particular the "torrid" one, bounded by the equinoctial lines of the Tropic of Cancer and the Tropic of Capricorn – comes in to play. This cartographic space, geographical imaginary, and, with the exploration of the African West Coast from the 1420s onwards also experiential space was preconfigured for Europeans by ancient Greek cosmography, geography, and ethnography. In other words, Herodotus', Ptolemy's, and Pliny's geographical accounts fully prepared Portuguese explorers to expect dark-skinned "Ethiopians" at the fringes of the "torrid zone", which was considered to be uninhabitable for its heat and barrenness. They also told of "Ethiopia", a vast and not clearly defined land of abundance beyond the Sahara (Cagle 2018, 128-129; Wey Gómez 2008, 74, 78). What started to emerge during the Portuguese exploration of the African West Coast, however, was that this lush land lay *inside* the space of the two equinoctial lines, in other words that healthy, abundant and, most of all, populated lands were to be found in the "torrid zone." So, while several of the ancient preconceptions seemed to be confirmed, an important geographical one – the torrid zone as being uninhabitable and barren – started to become unsettled already during the second half of the fifteenth century.

If we were to take the Curse of Ham story at face value and as the basis for how Europeans – or in our current case, Iberians – viewed dark-skinned Africans, we would have to infer that the Portuguese arrived in "Ethiopia" with the idea of their right to subjugate and enslave the peoples they encountered on the coasts of Guinea and what became known as the Gold and Ivory Coasts by dint of their skin color. Following Herman L. Bennett's powerful critique of postcolonial projections into the early modern history of the Portuguese African encounter, this was not the case. He argues that Portuguese African relations during the last half of the fifteenth century were shaped by the European recognition of authority and sovereignty of the "pagan" peoples they encountered. In conducting business with sometimes significant African kingdoms, the Portuguese often had to engage in diplomacy and politics contradictory to their own religious and legal customs. The extent to which these polities conformed to Iberian late medieval notions of sovereignty (based on Roman civil and canon law) informed who could be enslaved. Bennett demonstrates this relationship by a nuanced reading of the papal bull *Romanus Pontifex* (written in 1455), which confirmed Portuguese dominion over all lands (but not possession or dispossession of peoples) south of Cape Bajador (Bennett 2019, 84-85). This is not to argue that Iberians did not enslave Africans, but rather to clarify the notion under which enslavement of peoples was deemed possible in fifteenth and early sixteenth century European thought.

With regard to entanglement and the environment, it is clear how "Hippocratic environmentalism" and "Galenic humoralism" informed Portuguese expectations about humans and nature in the "torrid zone" in sailing beyond the previously known regions of the African West Coast. However, this preconceived knowledge, which included the identification of people to the very north and south of the habitable world as "barbarians," did not translate into simple manuals of oppression and enslavement. The important shift and the novelty occurred with regard to the kinds of environments and, consequently, resources that could be encountered "under the tropics" (*sub tropicis*).[12]

The riches the Portuguese acquired from their trade with sub-Saharan Africans did not remain hidden from the Spanish and therefore also the realization that to cross the Tropic of Cancer did not necessarily mean death and desolation through scorching heat. It could mean lush environments and precious metals, which the Spanish were urgently seeking. This shift in environmental perception and expectation of what to find "under the tropics" may also have informed Columbus' not only sailing west to find "India" but also his sailing *south*. Due to the Treaty of Alcaçovas (1479) between Portugal and Spain, which gave exclusive trading rights to the Portuguese in the Atlantic south of the Canary Islands, Columbus was in fact not allowed to sail south from those islands. According to

12 This expression is used by Bodin in *Methodus*, showing that by the 1560s, if not before, the "tropics" were considered a distinct region with specific (but throughout the unfolding European expansion also shifting) properties (Bodin 1566, 82).

Nicolás Wey Gómez' research, he tried to conceal his southern course from the Spanish crown as well as from the Portuguese King, because of the treaty and in order to protect his "discovery" from Portuguese claims until it was secured for Spain by the papal bull *Inter caetera* in May 1493 (Wey Gómez 2008, 313-314). Wey Gómez argues that with the "African tropics" in mind, Columbus sailed west *and south*, expecting to find dark-skinned people, abundant environments and silver and gold. Even though the people he encountered on the Caribbean islands did not match Columbus' tropical expectation with regard to skin color, he nevertheless portrayed them as inferior and cowardly (as shown in chapter 2) and therefore potentially "enslaveable" (ibid., 315).

Similar to what Bennett observes for African-Portuguese contact, Columbus projected late medieval understandings of authority and sovereignty onto these newfound lands. As he met with no opposition when he followed the official Iberian protocol of taking possession of land by raising the royal banner, he conjectured that the population of the Caribbean islands was under no discernible sovereignty. Neither did they claim possession of the land, therefore, according to the Christian logic, the population could be enslaved, and the land could be brought into the possession of the Spaniards (ibid., 319). So, even if the Curse of Ham had brought skin color and slavery together, the issue of sovereignty and rightful land lordship seems to have been more pervasive with regard to the question of enslavement at the turn to the sixteenth century.

However, apart from those political considerations of – in the European perspective – "unclaimed land," aspects pertaining to indigenous physique were also used as a justification for their enslavement. As we will see in a moment, in the Americas, these bodily aspects were pointing back to the environment and had, therefore, large-scale implications also for the Spaniards living there. Apart from pointing out that the Indians on Hispaniola went largely naked, the Spanish also noticed that the indigenous men did not grow beards. The Dominican Friar Gregorio García dedicated an extensive part of his treatise on the Origin of the Indians (*Origen de los indios del Nuevo Mundo*) published in 1607 to the reason why this was not the case. Much of his chapter on "why the Indios do not have beards" dwells on the question of the environment and whether it was the heat of the "torrid zone" that kept Indians from growing beards. They were compared with the "Ethiopians" who also lived in the torrid zone and also had no beards.

Next García brought up the concern whether it was possible that the Spaniards would lose their beards over time, living in this same environment as the Indians. The argument against such slow degeneration was made by suggesting that Spaniards could maintain their condition and their beards by eating European foods such as bread, wine and red meat. Another argument brought forth confined the problem more strongly to Indian bodies, rather than to the American environment. García made the humoral pathological argument that indigenous men were "of a humid nature, and they do not have enough natural heat which is required to overcome this humidity, therefore they do not have beards, like it happens with women, castrates and boys until they reach the age to procreate" (García 1607, 161). So, in addition to and in connection with the fact that the native foods were not properly nourishing (ibid., 154), Indian bodies, due to their excessive humidity were more like women's, therefore they did not grow facial hair and were generally not very strong and not "for much work" (ibid., 161). Clearly, beards as a sign of passing from boy- to manhood, were an indication of masculinity and virility for early modern Spaniards (see also Earle 2012, 24; Schiebinger 2004, chapter 4).

However, and importantly for our question of the nexus between dark skin and slavery, beards were also the sign of free men in early modern Spain, as Groebner remarks in his essay on complexion. "Among other things, it was the right to wear a beard that distinguished free male laborers from slaves in sixteenth- and seventeenth-century Italy and Spain" (Groebner 2004, 377). While I would not give too much credit to this factor in the question of what made some societies more "enslaveable" to early modern Iberians than others, it is nevertheless an interesting further piece of information. In particular in the light of Gregorio García's intertropical comparison between the beardless "Ethiopians" of Africa and the equally beardless "Indians" of America, both of whom had in fact been enslaved by Iberians in the course of the sixteenth century.

Along with Nicolás Wey Gómez who suggests that "tropicality" was already hard at work as an organizing principle in the earliest stages of Spanish expansion across the Atlantic, I would consider García's comparison as part of the ongoing process of defining this cartographic and geographic space. As has become clear so far, environmental factors either in the form of coveted resources and/or as an integral part of the late medieval/renaissance understanding of the cosmos, human health, and character are at the very basis of colonial, unequal relationships of power. This may seem obvious, however, for a large number of culturalist approaches to colonial history it is not. To quote Joyce Chaplin's still (or even more) acutely actual 2001 introduction to her book *Subject Matter: Technology, the Body, and Science on the Anglo-American Frontier, 1500-1676*: "Neglect of English theories of nature has imparted a sense that the English understood their place in the new world in terms divorced from the natural world, as if the intellectual history of early America had to do only with politics and religion" (Chaplin 2001, 10). This is equally true for the history of early Spanish America. Furthermore, with the example of Columbus' implicit assumption to expect similar riches to the west and south across the Atlantic as the Portuguese had encountered in the "torrid zone" of the African West Coast, we see again how practices of comparing become the driver for entangled history, or histories. Also, this implicit and initially non-discursive comparison of the "torrid zone" *sub tropicis* of the African West Coast with the one in the Americas, spells the beginning of the European construction of "the tropics."[13]

13 Wey Gómez sees the process of understanding "the tropics" as a distinct space already starting at the turn of the fifteenth century, while Hugh Cagle in his *Assembling the Tropics* perceives the concept of the tropics as coming into full relief (in particular in the context of medical history) only at the beginning of the eighteenth century (Cagle 2018, 803-804).

Let us return for a moment to the nexus of religion, "Hippocratic environmentalism"/"Galenic humoralism," slavery and the notion of race. That dark skin color was not a prerequisite for enslavement at the turn to the sixteenth century, despite the existence and spread of the curse of Ham, is also evidenced by the enslavement of the indigenous population of the Americas. Environmental factors such as the "humidity" outlined above that influenced the bodies and character of the indigenous population determined their "inferiority" and hence "enslaveability." However, if the American environment (including the new stars) could have such a degenerating effect on the native population who – after some initial reasoning on the side of the Spanish – was considered as having descended from Noah, it could have the same effect on the Spanish and their descendants who came to settle in the New World. Their bodies could degenerate and become effeminate to the degree of becoming "Indian." This effect could be staved off somewhat by eating European foods, as pointed out by García's tract and as elaborated by Rebecca Earle in her *Body of the Conquistador* (Earle 2012).

Jorge Cañizares Esguerra has described how this threat started to be discussed in a cross-Atlantic discourse throughout the sixteenth century. In particular, peninsular Spaniards could use the trope of the degenerate tropics against American *Criollos.* In this battle for superiority in how to interpret the American environment and *Criollo* character, Spanish Americans recast the malleability of the Indian and African body in the American tropics (Cañizares Esguerra 1999, 37; Cañizares Esguerra 2009a, 321-322). In order to maintain that American environments were *not* degenerate, yet at the same time to insist on the physical and mental inferiority of Amerindians, Spanish American creoles invented indigenous and African bodies that were ontologically different from theirs during the seventeenth century. In other words, a racialized discourse focusing on supposedly inherent differences between indigenous and creole bodies emerged from the mid-seventeenth century onwards in the Spanish colonies. This notion of "bodily difference along 'racial' lines" did however not spread back into the peninsular, let alone larger European discourse and hence, the idea of the porous body that could be changed by environmental conditions or astral constellations persisted (Cañizares Esguerra 2009a, 322). However, the process of hardening, racialized bodily categories was repeated on the island of Jamaica in the British colonial context during its evolution into a fully-fledged slave society during the seventeenth and eighteenth century, as Brooke Newman has shown in *A Dark Inheritance* (Newman 2018). The displacement of black Africans to regions outside of the tropics and the fact this did not change their skin color discredited "Hippocratic environmentalism's" explanatory force for skin color while curiously remaining intact to describe supposed moral differences between "tropical" and "temperate" peoples as exemplified by Joseph Renny's references to sloth and indolence at the beginning of this chapter.

The curse of Ham, connecting dark skin with slavery, as well as the curse of Issachar, which was employed by the Spanish to justify indigenous slavery, formed part of the justificatory repertoire of *Criollos* throughout the period outlined above (Cañizares Esguerra 2009a, 316; 2009b, 248). Even though David Goldenberg only localizes the curse of Ham in British America from 1700 onwards, it already arrived in the Americas with Spanish colonials and was used to justify African slavery at a moment of expansion of the Spanish empire during the mid-seventeenth century. Alonso de Sandoval, a Jesuit priest dedicated to the Christianization of enslaved Africans, justified their bondage chiefly by way of the curse of Ham, which he also explained by pointing to the fact that Cham was associated with *calidus*, Latin for "heat," that is, he invoked the environmental argument outlined earlier in this chapter (Almeida de Souza 2006, 16). Following Cañizares Esguerra's and other's (e.g. Seth 2018, 174ff.) argument about the waning influence of the environmental argument as a cause for different skin colors during the eighteenth century, it is possible to argue that the Christian/religious justification for slavery was enhanced while the "Hippocratic environmentalism" faded to the background.

## Adaptation, Pre-Adaptedness, and Acclimatization

By the mid-eighteenth century the discourse that whites could not perform hard labor under the conditions of the "torrid zone" had become widespread throughout the French and British colonial world. In other words, the image of the tropics as a dangerous and disease-ridden environment for (freshly arrived) Europeans had solidified by that time. Only Europeans who had lived in tropical environments or were even born there acquired a certain measure of protection from these dangerous conditions. However, despite this medical advantage, which usually referred to a certain resistance against tropical diseases, the image of the American or Caribbean white creole was still a negative one. The tropics had evolved to be seen as engendering lasciviousness, promiscuity, and laziness in its inhabitants (Arnold 1996a, 1996b; Livingstone 1991, 2002; Wey Gomez 2013; Osborne 2014; Newman 2018).

The question whether and how Europeans could live and maintain their health in these tropical climates was of as much interest to eighteenth century colonial regimes as it had been to the Spanish during the sixteenth and seventeenth century, not least in the context of war. Although one could argue that the concept of "adaptation" to an environment and climate (in the modern sense) is at the core of humoral pathology, the concept begins to appear increasingly in the eighteenth-century context of early tropical medicine. For example, the mortality of British troops stationed in occupied Saint Domingue during the early years of the Haitian Revolution (1791-1804), was discussed in terms of (non-)adaptation to the local climate by contemporaries. Hector McLean, Assistant Inspector of Hospitals in the British army, noted in a report that, as opposed to the freshly arrived British troops, "the French inhabitants were chiefly composed of people born in St. Domingo, and supported by that gradual adaptation to the climate, which habit confers on the natives of the most unhealthy regions" (McLean 1797, 13).

However, with the idea that the tropics were unhealthy for Europeans also came the notion of the pre-adaptedness[14] of Africans to those conditions by dint of having been born in the same meteorological zone, "under the climate of the tropics" and the by-then solidified notion of dark-skinned (tropical) peoples as slaves. This climatic (still in the pre-modern sense) argument for slavery became ubiquitous to justify the transatlantic slave trade in the eighteenth century. For example, in his *History of Jamaica*, Edward Long wrote about the relationship between the white colonizers and the enslaved Africans: "The just subordination, within the line of which our Negroes must be kept, does by no means dispense with our loving, and treating them humanely. We are obliged to, both from reason and self-interest; bodily strength, and their adaptation to the climate, would enable them to pass from the lowest to the highest stations [...]" (Long 1774, 2, 503-504). In other words, one reason to treat slaves humanely was because their physical features and their supposed pre-adaptedness to the climate enabled them to live and work in all parts of the island, which made them valuable "assets" for the colonists.

In a tract entitled *Idea del valor de la isla Española*, Santo Dominguan creole of color Antonio Sánchez Valverde outlines ways in which the Spanish part of the island of Hispaniola could be made economically valuable for the Spanish Crown. The island had experienced a long decline during the late sixteenth and the seventeenth century and had only started recuperating with the proper establishment of the French colony of Saint Domingue on the western

---

14 According to geographer William B. Meyer, the concept of preadaptation originated from the field of cultural geography in the 1970s, and has been applied most frequently to cases where population groups migrate from one environment to another. It points to the fact that "among the cultural traits that migrants carry with them, some will be well suited to the new environment. The migrants possessing those traits are described as preadapted to their new surroundings. They are likely to fare better there, other things being equal, than will other newcomers with traits poorly adapted to the new conditions" (Meyer 2000, 291).

side of the territory in 1697. Sánchez Valverde portrayed Saint Domingue, which at the point of his writing in the 1780s had already become the world's most valuable sugar colony, in shining colors. Quoting a French merchant's travel account (Weuves 1780), he outlined how Spanish Santo Domingo could become just like – or even better than – French Saint Domingue by understanding that "it is impossible to cultivate the soil of the *torrid zone* without *negroes*" and that "these burning climates do not permit *Europeans* to resist to the fatigues of their cultivation. All of them together would not be enough for this work. Only those who were born between the tropics can bear the excessive heat of the sun under its gradient" (Sánchez Valverde 1785, 148, original emphasis). In other words, the Spanish crown should invest in the massive importation of those enslaved Africans who were already "pre-adapted" to the conditions of Hispaniola.

Early eighteenth-century reports of the French engineers who built New Orleans and the fort *La Balize* at the mouth of the Mississippi abound with complaints about the weakness of whites who could not stand the tropical climate and the need for African slaves to build levees or fortifications. In January 1723, Engineer Le Blond de La Tour, for example, wrote to the Company of the Indies, which governed Louisiana between 1717 and 1731, that the plantation owners were asking for African slaves as "the whites which were sent cannot do anything since they lack French foodstuffs." And in September of the same year, De La Chaise, inspector of the Company, wrote to the directors that it was necessary that "good workers come [to the colony], for those who are here are useless and one even has to pay them 12 or 15 francs a day. Those in the service of the Company have been sick since we arrived and there is not one who has done any work [yet]."[15] Though the term adaptation is not used in these records, the preconceived notion that enslaved Afri-

15 Le Blond de La Tour to Directors, January 15, 1723, ANF, ANOM, Colonies, $C^{13}$ A 7, Fo. 197v.; De la Chaise to Directors, September 6, 1723, ANF, ANOM, Colonies, $C^{13}$ A 7, Fo. 16v.

cans would be better suited (and cheaper) for this work, comes across clearly in the colonial correspondence.

At the same time as the concept of adaptation came into use for humans and their environments, in France the term *acclimater* – to acclimatize – appeared in the context of the medical, agricultural and zoological discourse on colonizing Saint Domingue (Osborne 2000, 137). By 1798, the verb *acclimater* had found entry into the *Dictionnaire de l'Académie Française* and was defined as "to get accustomed to the temperature of a new climate" (Dictionnaire de l'Académie Française 1798). In France and Britain, throughout the eighteenth and the nineteenth century the theory of acclimatization developed into a science, which included transplanting plants, animals, and humans, into different climates. "Faith in the malleability of animal and plant form and function typified the French approach to acclimatization, and helps explain why the French attempted to introduce everything from ostriches to yaks and llamas both in their own country and in its dependencies." Acclimatization only lost its appeal after the diffusion of Louis Pasteur's germ theory and the progress in parasitological research on tropical diseases at the end of the nineteenth century (Osborne 2000, 139-140).

It appears, then, that the concept of "adaptation to an environment" (or climate) originated from the colonial experience of and discourse about European and African bodies "under the tropics" (*sub tropicis*). This is ironic and should give pause, given that the current climate crisis and its renewed use of this vocabulary was largely brought about by the emissions of Western "developed nations" whose very development was (and still is) built on the colonial exploitation of the tropics and its peoples. This is, however, only one of the ironies the Anthropocene creates with regard to the history of Western Modernity. Several others were pointed out by scholars such as Amitav Ghosh, Dipesh Chakrabarty, and Franz Mauelshagen (Chakrabarty 2009; Ghosh 2016; Mauelshagen 2017b).

During the sixteenth and seventeenth centuries, Spanish American creoles continued explaining the New World environment, peoples, and stars by comparing them with ancient Roman or Greek culture. By doing so, they assumed a likeness between Amerindians and Romans or Greeks, which in part occurred in the context of defending the Americas and themselves against peninsular Spaniards who considered them physically and mentally inferior for living in the "degenerate" environment of the Americas. These practices of comparing were rejected by Cornelius de Pauw and the Abbé Raynal in the eighteenth-century context of the "dispute of the New World." Spanish sources on the history of the Americas were dismissed by Europeans in this process and new interpretations of the American flora, fauna and humans were forged with comparisons in the American, British and French contexts of this debate (Cañizares Esguerra 2001, 38-49; Epple 2020; Gerbi 2010).

By following the genealogy of the *topoi* stated by Joseph Renny about enslaved Africans in the opening quotation of this chapter, it has become evident how much of this – by Renny's time more modern – racist thought was based on and had evolved from "Hippocratic environmentalism" and "Galenic humoralism" that conceived human bodies (including their skin color) as porous and adaptable to their environments. The evolution of the concept of race and racism cannot be properly understood without appreciating the role "the environment" – in its shifting meanings – plays in this (entangled) history.

Implicit and, in the beginning, non-discursive practices of comparing between the African "torrid zone" and the newly discovered American one, were driving the emergence of "the tropics" as a morally coded space and geopolitical imaginary (Epple and Kramer 2016), and continued to define this space through history. I would like to particularly emphasize the thematic nexus that evolved with these non-discursive and discursive practices of comparing. That is, when comparisons concerning the *comparatum* of the tropics were made, "climate" – first as a spatial and towards the nineteenth century as a meteorological category – the humoral effects it could have on the body (i.e. emasculation), and the status that ensued from this situation for peoples of tropical regions in the eyes of early modern

Europeans (i.e. inferiority and "enslaveability") were invoked along with the first *comparatum* without necessarily having to be made explicit. The binding link between those themes was "the environment," that is, "Hippocratic environmentalism"/"Galenic humoralism." Let me rephrase this idea by, again, pointing to Renny's quotation at the opening of this chapter. Though none of his statements is a comparison, they sit on top of four hundred-years' worth of comparative discourse about the tropics and slavery that would have been intelligible to contemporaries in their "Hippocratic environmental"/"Galenic humoral" dimension. I have only scratched at the very surface of these sediments of time, to invoke Reinhart Koselleck (Koselleck, Hoffmann, and Franzel 2018), more detailed and more primary source-based research needs to be done in order to expose the individual layers of these discursive sediments.

## 4. Conclusion: The Environment in Entanglement, and Practices of Comparing

This essay has covered the familiar ground of Columbus' "discovery" of the Americas and the partly familiar history of the concept of "race" and the body in the context of the enslavement of Africans and Indians in the Caribbean. However, I would argue that highlighting environmental factors in these familiar histories offers new perspectives on the past. It may have become evident throughout the case studies how difficult it is to try to operate with our present-day concepts of "environment" and "climate" in the late fifteenth, sixteenth and seventeenth centuries when these terms did either not exist yet or had an entirely different meaning. Inquiring into these environmental aspects of entangled histories requires a constant attuning and inquiring into what "environment" meant for contemporaries at specific points in time.

What is the added value, however, of bringing together the two conceptual perspectives I employed in this essay? How, if at all, are they connected? I argue that the perspective of environment-in-entanglement, allows for a broader and more realistic perspective on unequal (post-)colonial relationships of power and away from the view "as if the intellectual history of early America had to do only with politics and religion" or culture, for that matter (Chaplin 2001, 10). The factors of entanglement I have outlined in the introduction all point to the more "material" aspects of entangled histories, and the first case study, in particular, has shown how environmental factors are implicated in all of these four aspects (political power, migration, trade, and knowledge). It has also shown, that including environmental factors in the "material" sense, allows for a new reading of the "indigenous conspiracy" trope, and, by including the "archives of nature" (paleoclimatic records) may allow for a partial reconstruction of the past climatic and environmental conditions of those societies.

The approach of practices of comparing, however, is more strongly focused on discourse. As chapter 2 and 3 have shown, implicit and explicit practices of comparing were at the very core of the European Expansion of the late fifteenth and sixteenth century. And the central theme of these comparisons was "the environment," (broadly conceived) in the form of desirable and strange new resources and medicines, and, importantly, in the context of "Hippocratic environmentalism" and "Galenic humoralism" that informed Iberians expectations of what they might find towards the west and south across the Atlantic.

Understanding how this conception of "the environment" and the stars was entwined with a porous and adaptable human body is crucial. As chapter 3 has shown, with this cosmological perspective at the background, European discourses about the "nature of the Indian" or of "Ethiopians" are at the same time discourses about "the environment." In other words, concepts we have neatly separated in the present and that even belong to different (sometimes distant) disciplines such as medicine, biology, genetics, meteorology, and climate science, are united in the perspective of "Hippocratic environmentalism" and "Galenic humoralism."

This is not to say that the perspective of environment-in-entanglement cannot also unravel the discursive side of entangled histories. Yet, practices of comparing are able to capture in a unique way discourses that preceded and followed situations of cultural contact, conquest and colonization which were steeped in such "environmental comparisons." As we have seen *in nuce* in chapter 2, these "environmental comparisons" were repeated in similar, yet each time different fashion with every wave of colonizers in the Americas. The aspect that changes, is that later "newcomers" relied on and compared their experience against the accounts and information of earlier colonizers, as in the example of the English in Jamestown. The reason for the sustained meaningfulness of this practice of comparing environments (again, in the broadest sense) is the remarkable constancy of different elements of "Hippocratic environmentalism" and "Galenic humoralism," even into the nineteenth and early twentieth century.

That is, the perspective of practices of comparing in the context of the conquest of the Americas puts into sharp relief the layering of those sediments of discourse on the environment, climate (in the modern understanding) and peoples and how those sediments then fossilize into clichés over time as in the case of the nexus of environment, skin color, race and slavery. Needless to say, these clichés and established "truths" can become extremely effective drivers of historical processes. As explained at the end of chapter 3, these thematic clusters usually appear together, though they do not all need to be mentioned explicitly or even be part of an actual comparison as in Renny's quote at the beginning of chapter 3. This is how "tropicality" is constructed over time, starting with the Portuguese expansion to Africa and Columbus' journey west and south to "India," as Nicolás Wey Gómez has shown (Wey Gómez 2008).

In other words, practices of comparing are able to highlight an important and specific strand of entangled histories and the environment, namely the more culturally constructed side of these histories, whereas the environment-in-entanglement approach is able to zoom in on the "material" side of entanglement. Of course, both focuses can stand for themselves, however, combining them, in particular in the context of cultural contact conquest and colonization lends a breadth and balance that neither overemphasizes the constructivist aspect of history nor runs the risk of being environmentally determinist.

## Works Cited

Alberola Roma, Armando. 2014. *Los Cambios Climáticos. La Pequena Edad Del Hielo En Espana*. Madrid: Ediciónes Cátedra.

Albert, Mathias, Julia Engelschalt, Angelika Epple, Kai Kauffmann, Kerrin Langer, Malte Lorenzen, Torben Möbius, Thomas Müller, Leopold Ringel, Niko Rohé, Eleonora Rohland, Christopher Schulte-Schüren, Klaus Weinhauer, Thomas Welskopp, and Tobias Werron. 2019. "Vergleichen unter Bedingungen von Konflikt und Konkurrenz." *Working Paper des SFB 1288* 1.

Almeida de Souza, Juliana Beatriz. 2006. "Las Casas, Alonso De Sandoval and the Defence of Black Slavery." *Topoi (online edition)* 2.

Altman, Ida. 2007. "The Revolt of Enriquillo and the Historiography of Early Spanish America." *The Americas* 63, no. 4: 587-615.

Anderson-Córdova, Karen Frances. 2017. *Surviving Spanish Conquest: Indian Fight, Flight and Cultural Transformation in Hispaniola and Puerto Rico*. Tuscaloosa: The University of Alabama Press.

Anghiera, Pietro Martire d. 1555. *The Decades of the Newe Worlde or West India: Conteynyng the Nauigations and Conquestes of the Spanyardes….* Londini: In Aedibus Guilhelmi Powell.

Arnold, David. 1996a. *The Problem of Nature: Environment, Culture and European Expansion*. Oxford, Cambridge: Blackwell.

Arnold, David. 1996b. *Warm Climates and Western Medicine: The Emergence of Tropical Medicine, 1500-1900*. Amsterdam, Atlanta: Rodopi.

Aubert, Guillaume. 2004. "'The Blood of France'. Race and Purity of Blood in the French Atlantic World." *The William and Mary Quarterly* 61, no. 3: 439-478.

Bayly, Christopher Alan. 2004. *The Birth of the Modern World, 1780-1914: Global Connections and Comparisons*. Malden: Blackwell.

Behringer, Wolfgang. 2015. *Tambora und das Jahr ohne Sommer: Wie ein Vulkan die Welt in die Krise stürzte*. München: C.H. Beck.

Behringer, Wolfgang, Hartmut Lehmann and Christian Pfister, eds. 2005. *Kulturelle Konsequenzen der 'Kleinen Eiszeit'*. Göttingen: Vandenhoeck & Ruprecht.

Bennett, Herman L. 2019. *African Kings and Black Slaves: Sovereignty and Dispossession in the Early Modern Atlantic*. Philadelphia: University of Pennsylvania Press.

Bernhardt, Christoph. 2015. *Im Spiegel des Wassers: Eine transnationale Umweltgeschichte des Oberrheins (1800-2000)*. Köln: Böhlau.

Blackburn, Robin. 2010. *The Making of New World Slavery: From the Baroque to the Modern, 1492-1800*. London, New York: Verso.

Blanton, Dennis B. 2000. "Drought as a Factor in the Jamestown Colony, 1607-1612." *Historical Archaeology* 34, no. 4: 74-81.

Bleichmar, Daniela, Paula De Vos, Kristin Huffine, and Kevin Sheehan, eds. 2009. *Science in the Spanish and Portuguese Empires, 1500-1800*. Stanford: Stanford University Press.

Block, Sharon. 2018. *Colonial Complexions: Race and Bodies in Eighteenth-Century America*. Philadelphia: University of Pennsylvania Press.

Bodin, Jean. 1566. *Methodus ad Facilem Historiarum Cognitionem*. Parisiis: Apud Martinum Iuuenem.

Bodin, Jean. 1945. *Method for the Easy Comprehension of History*. Translated by Beatrice Reynolds. New York: Columbia University Press.

Borucki, Alex, David Eltis, and David Wheat. 2015. "Atlantic History and the Slave Trade to Spanish America." *The American Historical Review* 120, no. 2: 433-461.

Burn, Michael J., Jonathan Holmes, Lisa M. Kennedy, Allison Bain, Jim D. Marshall, and Sophia Perdikaris. 2016. "A Sediment-Based Reconstruction of Caribbean Effective Precipitation

During the 'Little Ice Age' from Freshwater Pond, Barbuda." *The Holocene* 26, no. 8: 1237-1247.

Burn, Michael J., and Suzanne E. Palmer. 2014. "Solar Forcing of Caribbean Drought Events During the Last Millennium." *Journal of Quaternary Science* 29, no. 8: 827-836.

Burn, Michael J., and Suzanne E. Palmer. 2015. "Atlantic Hurricane Activity During the Last Millennium." *Scientific Reports* 5: 12838.

Cagle, Hugh. 2018. *Assembling the Tropics: Science and Medicine in Portugal's Empire, 1450-1700.* Cambridge, New York, NY: Cambridge University Press.

Camenisch, Chantal. 2015. *Endlose Kälte: Witterungsverlauf und Getreidepreise in den Burgundischen Niederlanden im 15. Jahrhundert.* Basel: Schwabe.

Campbell, B. M. S. 2016. *The Great Transition: Climate, Disease and Society in the Late-Medieval World.* Cambridge, New York: Cambridge University Press.

Cañizares Esguerra, Jorge. 1999. "New World, New Stars: Patriotic Astrology and the Invention of Indian and Creole Bodies in Colonial Spanish America, 1600-1650." *The American Historical Review* 104, no. 1: 33-68.

Cañizares Esguerra, Jorge. 2001. *How to Write the History of the New World. Histories, Epistemologies, and Identities in the Eighteenth-Century Atlantic World.* Stanford: Stanford University Press.

Cañizares Esguerra, Jorge. 2009a. "Demons, Stars and the Imagination. The Early Modern Body in the Tropics." In *The Origins of Racism in the West.* Ben Isaac, Miriam Eliav-Feldon, and Yossi Ziegler (eds.), 313-325. Cambridge: Cambridge University Press.

Cañizares Esguerra, Jorge. 2009b. "Typology in the Atlantic World: Early Modern Readings of Colonization." In *Soundings in Atlantic History. Latent Structures and Intellectual Currents, 1500-1830.* Bernard Baylin and Patricia L. Denault (eds.), 237-264. Cambridge: Harvard University Press.

Carrera, Magali Marie. 2003. *Imagining Identity in New Spain: Race, Lineage, and the Colonial Body in Portraiture and Casta Paintings*. Austin: University of Texas Press.

Casas, Bartolomé de las, Feliciano Ramírez de Arellano Fuensanta del Valle, and José León Sancho Rayón. 1875 (1575). *Historia De Las Indias* (Vol. 2). Madrid: Imprenta de Miguel Ginesta.

Chakrabarty, Dipesh. 2009. "The Climate of History: Four Theses." *Critical Inquiry* 35, no. 2: 197-222.

Chaplin, Joyce E. 2001. *Subject Matter: Technology, the Body, and Science on the Anglo-American Frontier, 1500-1676*. Cambridge, London: Harvard University Press.

Chaplin, Joyce E. 2002. "Race." In *The British Atlantic World, 1500-1800*. David Armitage and Michael J. Braddick (eds.), 154-172. Basingstoke: Palgrave-Macmillan.

Cook, Noble David. 1993. "Disease and the Depopulation of Hispaniola 1492-1518." *Colonial Latin America Review* 2, no. 1-2: 211-245.

Cook, Noble David. 2002. "Sickness, Starvation, and Death in Early Hispaniola." *The Journal of Interdisciplinary History* 32, no. 3: 349-386.

Crosby, Alfred. 1986. *Ecolocigal Imperialism. The Biological Expansion of Europe, 900-1900*. Cambidge: Cambridge University Press.

Crosby, Alfred W. 1972. *The Columbian Exchange. Biological and Cultural Consequences of 1492*. Westport: Greenwood Press.

Crutzen, Paul J., and Eugene F. Stoermer. 2000. "The 'Anthropocene'." *International Geosphere-Biosphere Program (IGBP) Newsletter* 41: 17.

Curran, Andrew S. 2011. *The Anatomy of Blackness: Science and Slavery in an Age of Enlightenment*. Baltimore: Johns Hopkins University Press.

Deagan, Kathleen A. 2010. "Native American Resistance to Spanish Presence in Hispaniola and La Florida, ca. 1492-1650." In *Enduring Conquests. Rethinking the Archaeology of Resistance to Spanish Colonialim in the Americas*. Matthew Liebmann and

Melissa S. Murphy (eds.), 41-56. Santa Fe: School for Advanced Research Press.

Deagan, Kathleen, and J. O. S. Cruxent. 2002. "Reluctant Hosts. The Taínos of Hispaniola." In *Columbus's Outpost among the Taínos. Spain and America at La Isabela, 1493-1498.* Kathleen Deagan and J. O. S. Cruxent (eds.), 23-46. New Haven: Yale University Press.

Delbourgo, James, and Nicholas Dew, eds. 2008. *Science and Empire in the Atlantic World.* New York: Routledge.

Dictionnaire de l'Académie Française. 1798. "Acclimater". In *Dictionnaire de l'Académie Française* (5th ed.). University of Chicago: ARTFL Encyclopédie Project (Spring 2011) (ed.). http://encyclopedie.uchicago.edu/, accessed December 12, 2019.

Dueck, Daniela, and Kai Brodersen. 2012. *Geography in Classical Antiquity.* Cambridge: Cambridge University Press.

Earle, Rebecca. 2010. "'If You Eat Their Food ...': Diets and Bodies in Early Colonial Spanish America." *The American Historical Review* 115, no. 3: 688-713.

Earle, Rebecca. 2012. *The Body of the Conquistador: Food, Race, and the Colonial Experience in Spanish America, 1492-1700.* Cambridge, New York: Cambridge University Press.

Eltis, David. 1997. *Routes to Slavery. Direction, Ethnicity and Mortality in the Transatlantic Slave Trade.* London: Cass.

Eltis, David. 2000. *The Rise of African Slavery in the Americas.* Cambridge: Cambridge University Press.

Eltis, David, and Martin Halbert. 2013. The Transatlantic Slave Trade Database. Retrieved from https://www.slavevoyages.org/, accessed December 30, 2019.

Eltis, David, and David Richardson. 2010. *Atlas of the Transatlantic Slave Trade.* New Haven, London: Yale University Press.

Eltis, David, Frank D. Lewis, and Kimberly McIntyre. 2010. "Accounting for the Traffic in Africans: Transport Costs on Slaving Voyages." *The Journal of Economic History* 70, no. 4: 940-963.

Emile-Geay, Julien, Kimberly M. Cobb, Michael E. Mann, and Andrew T. Wittenberg. 2013. "Estimating Central Equatorial

Pacific Sst Variability over the Past Millennium. Part II: Reconstructions and Implications." *Journal of Climate* 26, no. 7: 2329-2352.

Epple, Angelika. 2015. "Doing Comparisons: Ein praxeologischer Zugang zur Geschichte der Globalisierung/en." In *Die Welt beobachten: Praktiken des Vergleichens.* Angelika Epple and Walter Erhart (eds.), 161-202. Frankfurt am Main: Campus Verlag.

Epple, Angelika. 2020. "Comparing Europe and the Americas: The Dispute of the New World between the Sixteenth and Nineteenth Centuries." In *The Force of Comparisons. A New Perspective on Modern European History and the Contemporary World.* Willibald Steinmetz (ed.), 137-163. New York: Berghahn Books.

Epple, Angelika, and Walter Erhart, ed. 2015. *Die Welt beobachten: Praktiken des Vergleichens*. Frankfurt am Main: Campus Verlag.

Epple, Angelika, and Kirsten Kramer. 2016. "Globalization, Imagination, Social Space: The Making of Geopolitical Imaginaries." *Forum for Inter-American Research FIAR* 9, no. 1: 41-63.

Epple, Angelika, and Ulrike Lindner. 2011. "Introduction: Entangled Histories. Reflecting on Concepts of Coloniality and Postcoloniality." *Comparativ. Zeitschrift für Globalgeschichte und Vergleichende Gesellschaftsgeschichte* 21, no. 1: 7-13.

Evers, Hans Dieter. 1986. "Subsistenzproduktion, Markt und Staat: Der sogenannte Bielefelder Ansatz." *Bielefeld University: Sociology of Development Research Centre. Working Papers*, no. 85: 1-15.

Fernández de Oviedo y Valdés, Gonzalo. 1535. *Historia General Y Natural De Las Indias*. London: King's College London.

Fernandez de Oviedo y Váldez, Gonzalo. 1851 (1535). *Historia General Y Natural De Las Indias: Islas Y Tierra Firme Del Mar Océano*. Madrid: Real Academia de la Historia.

Feros, Antonio. 2017. *Speaking of Spain: The Evolution of Race and Nation in the Hispanic World.* Cambridge, Massachusetts: Harvard University Press.

Funes Monzote, Reinaldo. 2008. *De Los bosques a los cañaverales: Una historia ambiental de Cuba 1491-1926.* La Habana: Editorial de Ciencias Sociales.

Fuson, Robert Henderson. 1992. *The Log of Christopher Columbus.* New York: International Marine Publishing, 1992

Gailus, Manfred. 2001. "Die Erfindung des 'Korn-Juden'. Zur Geschichte eines antijüdischen Feindbildes des 18. und 19. Jahrhunderts." *Historische Zeitschrift* 272: 597-622.

García, Gregorio. 1607. *Origen de Los Indios de el Nuevo Mundo, e Indias occidentales, averiguado con discurso de opiniones.* Valencia: Pedro Patricio Mey.

Gerbi, Antonello. 2010. *The Dispute of the New World. The History of a Polemic, 1750-1900.* Translated by Jeremy Moyle. Pittsburgh: University of Pittsburgh Press.

Ghosh, Amitav. 2016. *The Great Derangement: Climate Change and the Unthinkable.* Chicago: Chicago University Press.

Girolamo, Vittorio. 1609. "Raça". In *Tesoro, de las tres lenguas francesa, italiana y española. Thresor des trois langues françoise, italienne et espagnolle.* Ginebra: Philippe Albert and Alexandre Pernet.

Goldenberg, David. 2003. *The Curse of Ham: Race and Slavery in Early Judaism, Christianity, and Islam.* Princeton: Princeton University Press.

Goldenberg, David. 2017. *Black and Slave: The Origins and History of the Curse of Ham.* Berlin: De Gruyter.

Groebner, Valentin. 2004. "Complexio/Complexion: Categorizing Individual Natures, 1250-1600." In *The Moral Authority of Nature.* Lorraine Daston and Fernando Vidal (eds.), 361-383. Chicago: Chicago University Press.

Grove, Richard and George Adamson. 2018. *El Niño in World History.* London: Palgrave McMillan.

Grove, Richard H. 1996. *Green Imperialism. Colonial Expansion, Tropical Island Edens and the Origins of Environmentalism 1600-1860*. Cambridge: Cambridge University Press.

Hanger, Kimberly. 1993. "Conflicting Loyalties: The French Revolution and Free People of Color in Spanish New Orleans." *Louisiana History: The Journal of the Louisiana Historical Association* 34, no. 1: 5-33.

Hannaford, Matthew J. 2018. "Long-Term Drivers of Vulnerability and Resilience to Drought in the Zambezi-Area of Southern Africa, 1505-1830." *Global and Planetary Change* 166: 94-106.

Hannaford, Matthew J., and David J. Nash. 2016. "Climate, History, Society over the Last Millennium in Southeast Africa." *WIRES Climate Change* 7, no. 3: 370-392.

Hensley, Nathan K., and Philip Steer. 2019. *Ecological Form. System and Aesthetics in the Age of Empire*. New York: Fordham University Press.

Jankovic, Vladimir. 2000. *Reading the Skies. A Cultural History of the English Weather, 1650-1820*. Manchester: Manchester University Press.

Kaltmeier, Olaf, Ulrike Lindner, and Binu Mailaparambil. 2011. "Reflecting on Concepts of Coloniality/Postcoloniality in Latin American, South Asian and African Historiography." *Comparativ. Zeitschrift für Globalgeschichte und Vergleichende Gesellschaftsgeschichte* 21, no. 1: 14-31.

Kay, Cristóbal. 1989. *Latin American Theories of Development and Underdevelopment*. London etc.: Routledge.

Klein, Herbert S., and Ben Vinson. 2007. *African Slavery in Latin America and the Caribbean*. Oxford, New York: Oxford University Press.

Kocka, Jürgen. 2001. "Einladung zur Diskussion." *Geschichte und Gesellschaft* 27, no. 3: 463.

Koselleck, Reinhart, Stefan-Ludwig Hoffmann, and Sean Franzel. 2018. *Sediments of Time: On Possible Histories*. Stanford, CA: Stanford University Press.

Kupper, Patrick. 2014. *Creating Wilderness. A Transnational History of the Swiss National Park.* New York: Berghahn Books.

Kupperman, Karen Ordahl. 1979. "Apathy and Death in Early Jamestown." *The Journal of American History* 66, no. 1: 24-40.

Kupperman, Karen Ordahl. 1982. "The Puzzle of the American Climate in the Early Colonial Period." *American Historical Review* 87, no. 5: 1262-1289.

Kupperman, Karen Ordahl. 1984. "Fear of Hot Climates in the Anglo-American Colonial Experience." *William and Mary Quarterly* 41, no. 2: 213-240.

Kupperman, Karen Ordahl. 2007. *The Jamestown Project.* Cambridge, MA: Belknap Press of Harvard University Press.

Lane, Chad S., Sally P. Horn, Kenneth H. Orvis, and John M. Thomason. 2011. "Oxygen Isotope Evidence of Little Ice Age Aridity on the Caribbean Slope of the Cordillera Central, Dominican Republic." *Quaternary Research* 75, no. 3: 461-470.

Livi Bacci, Massimo. 2008. *Conquest: The Destruction of the American Indios*. Cambridge: Polity Press.

Livingstone, David N. 1991. "The Moral Discourse of Climate: Historical Considerations on Race, Place and Virtue." *Journal of Historical Geography* 17, no. 4: 413-434.

Livingstone, David N. 2002. "Race, Space and Moral Climatology: Notes toward a Genealogy." *Journal of Historical Geography* 28, no. 2: 159-180.

Long, Edward. 1774. *The History of Jamaica or General Survey of the Antient and Modern State of That Island with Reflections on Its Situation, Settlement, Inhabitants, Climate, Products, Commerce, Laws, and Governments* (Vol. III). London: T. Lowndes.

Malaizé, B., P. Bertran, P. Carbonel, D. Bonnissent, K. Charlier, D. Galop, D. Imbert, N. Serrand, Ch. Stouvenot, C. Pujol. 2011. "Hurricanes and Climate in the Caribbean During the Past 3700 Years Bp." *The Holocene* 21, no. 6: 911-924, DOI: 10.1177/0959683611400198.

Mandelblatt, Bertie. 2008. "Beans from Rochel and Manioc from Prince's Island: West Africa, French Atlantic Commodity Circuits, and the Provisioning of the French Middle Passage." *History of European Ideas* 34: 411-423.

Mandelblatt, Bertie. 2013. "How Feeding Slaves Shaped the French Atlantic: Mercantilism and the Crisis of Food Provisioning in the Franco-Caribbean During the Seventeenth and Eighteenth Centuries." In *The Political Economy of Empire in the Early Modern World.* Sophus Reinert and Pernille Røge (eds.), 192-220. Basingstoke: Palgrave Macmillan.

Mandelblatt, Bertie. 2016. "'A Land Where Hunger Is in Gold and Famine Is in Opulence:' Plantation Slavery, Island Ecology, and the Fear of Famine in the French Caribbean." In *Fear and the Shaping of Early American Societies.* Lauric Henneton and Lyndal H. Roper (eds.), 243-264. Leiden: Brill.

Margry, Pierre. 1881. *Découvertes Et Établissements Des Français Dans L'ouest Et Dans Le Sud De L'amérique Septentrionale (1614-1754). Mémoires Et Documents Originaux. Découverte Par Mer Des Bouches Du Mississippi Et Établissments De Le Moyne D'iberville Sur Le Golfe Du Méxique (1694-1703)* (Vol. 4). Paris: Maisonneuve et Cie.

Matei-Chesnoiu, Monica. 2015. *Geoparsing Early Modern English Drama.* New York: Palgrave Macmillan US.

Mauelshagen, Franz. 2010. *Klimageschichte der Neuzeit 1500-1900.* Darmstadt: WBG.

Mauelshagen, Franz. 2011. *Wunderkammer auf Papier. Die 'Wickiana' zwischen Reformation und Volksglaube.* Epfendorf: Bibliotheca Academica Verlag.

Mauelshagen, Franz. 2017a. "Anthropozän." In *Staatslexikon* (8th ed.), Vol. 1, 241-244. Freiburg i. Br.: Herder.

Mauelshagen, Franz. 2017b. "Bridging the Great Divide. The Anthropocene as a Challenge to the Social Sciences and Humanities." In *Religion and the Anthropocene.* Celia Deane-Drummond, Markus Vogt, and Sigurd Bergmann (eds.), 87-102. Eugene, OR: Lutterworth Press.

Mauelshagen, Franz. 2017c. "Reflexiones Acerca Del Anthropoceno." *Desacatos* 54: 74-89.

Mauelshagen, Franz. 2018. "Climate as a Scientific Paradigm – Early History of Climatology to 1800." In *The Palgrave Handbook of Climate History.* Sam White, Christian Pfister, and Franz Mauelshagen (eds.), 565-588. Basingstoke: Palgrave Macmillan.

Mauelshagen, Franz. 2019. "Die große Stoffwechselanomalie." In *Transformationsgesellschaften.* Michaela Christ, Bernd Sommer, and Klara Stumpf (eds.), 18-46. Weimar: Metropolis.

Mauelshagen, Franz. 2020. "The Dirty Metaphysics of Fossil Freedom." In *The Anthropocenic Turn: Interplay Between Disciplinary and Interdisciplinary Responses to a New Age*, Gabriele Dürbeck, and Philip Hüpkes (eds.), 59-76. New York: Routledge, 2020

McClellan, James E. 2010. *Colonialism and Science. Saint Domingue in the Old Regime.* Baltimore: Johns Hopkins University Press.

McCook, Stuart. 2002. *States of Nature: Science, Agriculture, and Environment in the Spanish Caribbean, 1760-1940.* Austin: University of Texas Press.

McCook, Stuart. 2011. "The Neo-Columbian Exchange: The Second Conquest of the Greater Caribbean, 1720-1930." *Latin American Research Review* 46: 11-31.

McLean, Hector. 1797. *An Enquiry into the Nature and Causes of the Great Mortality among the Troops at St. Domingo. With Practical Remarks on the Fever of That Island and Directions for the Conduct of Europeans on Their First Arrival in Warm Climates* London: Printed for T. Cadell Jun. and W. Davies.

McNeill, John R. 2010. *Mosquito Empires: Ecology and War in the Greater Caribbean, 1620-1914.* Cambridge: Cambridge University Press.

Meyer, William B. 2000. "Appendix A: Climate and Migration." In *The Role of Migration in the History of the Eurasian Steppe.*

*Sedentary Civilization vs. "Barbarian" and Nomad.* Andrew Bell-Fialkoff (ed.), 287-294. New York: St. Martin's Press.

Middell, Matthias. 2000. "Kulturtransfer und historische Komparatistik. Thesen zu ihrem Verhältnis." *Comparativ. Zeitschrift für Globalgeschichte und Vergleichende Gesellschaftsgeschichte* 10, no. 1: 7-41.

Millás, José Carlos, and Leonard Pardue. 1968. *Hurricanes of the Caribbean and Adjacent Regions, 1492-1800.* Miami, FL: Academy of the Arts and Sciences of the Americas.

Mira Caballos, Esteban. 1997. *El Indio Antillano. Repartimiento, Encomienda Y Esclavitud (1492-1542).* Sevilla: Munoz Moya Editora.

Moya Pons, Frank, and Rosario Flores Paz, eds. (2013). *Los taínos en 1492. El debate demográfico.* Santo Domingo: Academia Dominicana de la Historia.

Navarrete, Martín Fernández de. 1825. *Coleccion De Los Viajes Y Descubrimientos Que Hicieron Por Mar Los Españoles Desde Fines Del Siglo Xv Con Varios Documentos Inéditos Concernientes À La Historia De La Marina Castellana Y De Los Establecimientos Españoles En Indias.* Madrid: Imprenta Nacional.

Newman, Brooke N. 2018. *A Dark Inheritance: Blood, Race, and Sex in Colonial Jamaica.* New Haven: Yale University Press.

Osborne, Michael A. 2000. "Acclimatizing the World. A History of the Paradigmatic Colonial Science." *Osiris* 15: 135-151.

Osborne, Michael A. 2014. *The Emergence of Tropical Medicine in France.* Chicago: University of Chicago Press.

Parker, Geoffrey. 1983. "Die Entstehung des modernen Geld- und Finanzwesens in Europa 1500-1730." In *Europäische Wirtschaftsgeschichte.* Carlo M. Cipolla, and Knut Borchardt (eds.), Vol. 2, 335-379. Stuttgart: Gustav Fischer Verlag.

Parry, John H., and Robert J. Keith, ed. (1984). *New Iberian World. A Documentary History of the Discovery and Settlement of Latin America to the Early 17th Century. Vol. 1: The Con-*

*querors and the Conquered.* New York: The New York Times Books.

Pfister, Christian. 2007. "Climatic Extremes, Recurrent Crises and Witch Hunts. Strategies of European Societies in Coping with Exogenous Shocks in the Late Sixteenth and Early Seventeenth Centuries." *Medieval History Journal* 10: 33-73.

Pfister, Christian, and Rudolf Brázdil. 1999. "Climatic Variability in Sixteenth-Century Europe and Its Social Dimension: A Synthesis." *Climatic Change* 43: 5-53.

Pfister, Christian, and Rudolf Brázdil. 2006. "Social Vulnerability to Climate in the 'Little Ice Age.' An Example from Central Europe in the Early 1770s." *Climate of the Past Discussions* 2: 123-155.

Pribyl, Kathleen. 2017. *Farming, Famine and Plague. The Impact of Climate in Late Medieval England.* Cham: Springer.

Raudzens, George. 1996. "Why Did Amerindian Defences Fail? Parallels in the European Invasions of Hispaniola, Virginia and Beyond." *War in History* 3, no. 3: 331-352.

Reinhard, Wolfgang. 2016. *Die Unterwerfung der Welt. Globalgeschichte der europäischen Expansion 1415-2015*. München: C. H. Beck.

Renny, Robert. 1807. *An History of Jamaica: With Observations on the Climate, Scenery, Trade, Productions, Negroes, Slave Trade, Diseases of Europeans, Customs, Manners, and Dispositions of the Inhabitants: To Which Is Added, an Illustration of the Advantages Which Are Likely to Result from the Abolition of the Slave Trade*. London: Printed for J. Cawthorn.

Rockman, Marcy. 2003. "Knowledge and Learning in the Archaeology of Colonization." In *Colonization of Unfamiliar Landscapes. The Archaeology of Adaptation.* Marcy Rockman, and James Steele (eds.), 3-24. New York: Routledge.

Rohland, Eleonora. 2016. "Hurricanes on the Gulf Coast: Environmental Knowledge and Science in Louisiana, the Caribbean, and the U.S., 1722-1900." In *Works of Nature: Global Scientific Practice During the Age of Revolutions.* Daniel Rood and

Patrick Manning (eds.), 38-53. Pittsburgh: University of Pittsburgh Press.

Rohland, Eleonora. 2017. "Adapting to Hurricanes. A Historical Perspective on New Orleans from Its Foundation to Hurricane Katrina, 1718-2005." *WIRES Climate Change.* DOI: 10.1002/wcc.1488.

Rohland, Eleonora. 2019. *Changes in the Air. Hurricanes in New Orleans from 1718 to the Present.* Oxford, New York: Berghahn Books.

Rohland, Eleonora, Angelika Epple, Antje Flüchter, and Kirsten Kramer, eds. 2021. *Contact, Conquest, and Colonization: How Practices of Comparing Shaped Empires and Colonialism around the World.* New York: Routledge.

Rütten, Markus. 2012. "Early Modern Medicine." In *The Oxford Handbook of the History of Medicine.* Mark Jackson (ed.), 60-81. Oxford: Oxford University Press.

Said, Edward W. 1978. *Orientalism.* London: Routledge and Kegan Paul.

Sánchez Valverde, Antonio. 1785. *Idea Del Valor De La Isla Española, Y Utilidades, Que De Ella Puede Sacar Su Monarquia.* Madrid: Don Pedro Marin.

Sauer, Carl Ortwin. 1966. *The Early Spanish Main.* Berkeley: University of California Press.

Schiebinger, Londa L. 2004. *Nature's Body: Gender in the Making of Modern Science.* New Brunswick, N.J.: Rutgers University Press.

Schiebinger, Londa L. 2017. *Secret Cures of Slaves: People, Plants, and Medicine in the Eighteenth-Century Atlantic World.* Stanford, CA: Stanford University Press.

Schulz, Raimund. 2016. *Abenteurer der Ferne. Die großen Entdeckungsfahrten und das Weltwissen der Antike.* Stuttgart: Klett-Kotta.

Schwartz, Stuart B. 2004. *Tropical Babylons: Sugar and the Making of the Atlantic World, 1450-1680.* Chapel Hill: University of North Carolina Press.

Seth, Suman. 2014. “Materialism, Slavery, and the History of Jamaica.” *Isis* 105, no. 4: 764-772.

Seth, Suman. 2018. *Difference and Disease. Medicine, Race, and the Eighteenth-Century British Empire.*

Sheridan, Richard B. 1976. “The Crisis of Slave Subsistence in the British West Indies During and after the American Revolution.” *William and Mary Quarterly* 33, no. 4: 615-641.

Siraisi, Nancy G. 1990. *Medieval and Early Renaissance Medicine: An Introduction to Knowledge and Practice.* Chicago: University of Chicago Press.

Smith, John, Edward Arber, and A. G. Bradley. 1910. *Travels and Works of Captain John Smith President of Virginia and Admiral of New England, 1580-1631.* Edinburgh: John Grant.

Steffen, Will, Jacques Grinevald, Paul Crutzen, and John R. McNeill. 2011. “The Anthropocene. Conceptual and Historical Perspectives.” *Philosophical Transactions of the Royal Society A: Mathematical, Physical and Engineering Sciences* 369: 842-867.

Subrahmanyam, Sanjay. 1997. “Connected Histories: Notes Towards a Reconfiguration of Early Modern Eurasia.” *Modern Asian Studies* 31, no. 3: 735-762.

Tyrrell, Ian R. 1991. “American Exceptionalism in an Age of International History.” *American Historical Review* 96, no. 4: 1031-1055.

Walker, Mike, Sigfus Johnsen, Sune Olander Rasmussen, Trevor Popp, Jørgen-Peder Steffensen, Phil Gibbard, Wim Hoek, et al. 2009. “Formal definition and dating of the GSSP (Global Stratotype Section and Point) for the base of the Holocene using the Greenland NGRIP ice core, and selected auxiliary records.” *Journal of Quaternary Science* 24, no. 1: 3-17

Wallerstein, Immanuel Maurice. 1974. *The Modern World-System.* New York, N.Y.: Academic Press.

Watts, David. 1984. “Cycles of Famine in Islands of Plenty: The Case of the Colonial West Indies in the Pre-Emancipation Period.” In *Famine as a Geographical Phenomenon.* Bruce

Currey and Graeme Hugo (eds.), 49-70. Dordrecht: D. Reidel Publishing Company.

Werner, Michael, and Bénédicte Zimmermann. 2002. "Vergleich, Transfer, Verflechtung. Der Ansatz der Histoire croisée und die Herausforderung des Transnationalen." *Geschichte und Gesellschaft* 28, no. 4: 607-636.

Werner, Michael, and Bénédicte Zimmermann. 2006. "Beyond Comparison. Histoire Croisée and the Challenge of Reflexivity." *History and Theory* 45, no. February: 30-50.

Weuves, M. 1780. *Réflexions historiques et politiques sur le commerce de France avec ses colonies de l'Amérique*. Paris: L. Cellot.

Wey Gómez, Nicolás. 2013. "Memorias De La Zona Tórrida: El Naturalismo Clásico Y La 'Tropicalidad' Americana En El Sumario De La Natural Historia De Las Indias De Gonzalo Fernández De Oviedo (1526)." *Revista de Indias* 73, no. 259: 609-632.

Wey Gómez, Nicolás. 2008. *The Tropics of Empire: Why Columbus Sailed South to the Indies*. Cambridge: MIT Press.

White, Richard. 1999. "The Nationalization of Nature." *Journal of American History* 86, no. 3: 976-986.

White, Sam, Christian Pfister, and Franz Mauelshagen, ed. 2018. *Palgrave Handbook of Climate History*. Basingstoke: Palgrave Macmillan.

Wilson, Samuel Meredith. 1990. *Hispaniola: Caribbean Chiefdoms in the Age of Columbus*. Tuscaloosa: University of Alabama Press.

Worster, Donald. 1982. "World without Borders: The Internationalizing of Environmental History." *Environmental History* 6, no. 2: 8-13.

# INTER-AMERICAN STUDIES
## Cultures – Societies – History

# ESTUDIOS INTERAMERICANOS
## Culturas – Sociedades – Historia

This interdisciplinary series examines national and transnational issues in the cultures, societies, and histories of the Americas. It creates a forum for a critical academic dialogue between North and South, promoting an inter-American paradigm that shifts the scholarly focus from methodological nationalism to the wider context of the Western Hemisphere.

Vol. 1
Raab, Josef, Sebastian Thies, and Daniela Noll-Opitz, eds. *Screening the Americas: Narration of Nation in Documentary Film / Proyectando las Américas: Narración de la nación en el cine documental.* 2011. 470 pp.

| | | |
|---|---|---|
| WVT Wissenschaftlicher Verlag Trier | ISBN 978-3-86821-331-7 | € 29,50 |
| Bilingual Press / Editorial Bilingüe | ISBN 978-1-931010-83-2 | $ 29.50 |

Vol. 2
Raussert, Wilfried, and Michelle Habell-Pallán, eds. *Cornbread and Cuchifritos: Ethnic Identity Politics, Transnationalization, and Transculturation in American Urban Popular Music.* 2011. 292 pp.

| | | |
|---|---|---|
| WVT Wissenschaftlicher Verlag Trier | ISBN 978-3-86821-265-5 | € 29,50 |
| Bilingual Press / Editorial Bilingüe | ISBN 978- 1-931010-80-1 | $ 29.50 |

Vol. 3
Butler, Martin, Jens Martin Gurr, and Olaf Kaltmeier, eds. *EthniCities: Metropolitan Cultures and Ethnic Identities in the Americas.* 2011. 268 pp.

| | | |
|---|---|---|
| WVT Wissenschaftlicher Verlag Trier | ISBN 978-3-86821-310-2 | € 29,50 |
| Bilingual Press / Editorial Bilingüe | ISBN 978-1-931010-81-8 | $ 29.50 |

Vol. 4
Gurr, Jens Martin, and Wilfried Raussert, eds. *Cityscapes in the Americas and Beyond: Representations of Urban Complexity in Literature and Film.* 2011. 300 pp.

| | | |
|---|---|---|
| WVT Wissenschaftlicher Verlag Trier | ISBN 978-3-86821-324-9 | € 29,50 |
| Bilingual Press / Editorial Bilingüe | ISBN 978-1-931010-82-5 | $ 29.50 |

Vol. 5

Kirschner, Luz Angélica, ed. *Expanding* Latinidad*: An Inter-American Perspective.* 2012. 292 pp.

WVT Wissenschaftlicher Verlag Trier ISBN 978-3-86821-309-6 € 29,50
Bilingual Press / Editorial Bilingüe ISBN 978-1-931010-84-9 $ 29.50

Vol. 6

Raussert, Wilfried, and Graciela Martínez-Zalce, eds. *(Re)Discovering 'America': Road Movies and Other Travel Narratives in North America / (Re)Descubriendo 'América': Road movie y otras narrativas de viaje en América del Norte.* 2012. 252 pp.

WVT Wissenschaftlicher Verlag Trier ISBN 978-3-86821-384-3 € 29,50
Bilingual Press / Editorial Bilingüe ISBN 978-1-931010-91-7 $ 29.50

Vol. 7

Kaltmeier, Olaf, ed. *Transnational Americas: Envisioning Inter-American Area Studies in Globalization Processes*. 2013. 278 pp.

WVT Wissenschaftlicher Verlag Trier ISBN 978-3-86821-415-4 € 29,50
Bilingual Press / Editorial Bilingüe ISBN 978-1-931010-92-4 $ 29.50

Vol. 8

Raab, Josef, and Alexander Greiffenstern, eds. *Interculturalism in North America: Canada, the United States, Mexico, and Beyond.* 2013. 312 pp.

WVT Wissenschaftlicher Verlag Trier ISBN 978-3-86821-460-4 € 29,50
Bilingual Press / Editorial Bilingüe ISBN 978-1-931010-99-3 $ 29.50

Vol. 9

Raab, Josef, ed. *New World Colors: Ethnicity, Belonging, and Difference in the Americas*. 2014. 418 pp.

WVT Wissenschaftlicher Verlag Trier ISBN 978-3-86821-461-1 € 29,50
Bilingual Press / Editorial Bilingüe ISBN 978-1-939743-00-8 $ 39.50

Vol. 10

Roth, Julia. *Occidental Readings, Decolonial Practices: A Selection on Gender, Genre, and Coloniality in the Americas*. 2014. 284 pp.

WVT Wissenschaftlicher Verlag Trier ISBN 978-3-86821-446-8 € 26,50
Bilingual Press / Editorial Bilingüe ISBN 978-1-939743-07-7 $ 32.50

Vol. 11

Thies, Sebastian, Gabriele Pisarz-Ramirez, and Luzelena Gutiérrez de Velasco, eds. *Of Fatherlands and Motherlands: Gender and Nation in the Americas / De Patrias y Matrias: Género y nación en las Américas*. 2015. 344 pp.

WVT Wissenschaftlicher Verlag Trier ISBN 978-3-86821-528-1 € 29,50
Bilingual Press / Editorial Bilingüe ISBN 978-1-939743-08-4 $ 39.50

Vol. 12
Fuchs, Rebecca. *Caribbeanness as a Global Phenomenon: Junot Díaz, Edwidge Danticat, and Cristina García*. 2014. 298 pp.
WVT Wissenschaftlicher Verlag Trier ISBN 978-3-86821-533-5 € 26,50
Bilingual Press / Editorial Bilingüe ISBN 978-1-939743-09-1 $ 32.50

Vol. 13
Andres, Julia. *¡Cuéntame algo! – Chicana Narrative Beyond the Borderlands*. 2015. 202 pp.
WVT Wissenschaftlicher Verlag Trier ISBN 978-3-86821-569-4 € 25,00
Bilingual Press / Editorial Bilingüe ISBN 978-1-939743-11-4 $ 28.50

Vol. 14
Hertlein, Saskia. *Tales of Transformation: Emerging Adulthood, Migration, and Ethnicity in Contemporary American Literature*. 2014. 228 pp.
WVT Wissenschaftlicher Verlag Trier ISBN 978-3-86821-570-0 € 25,00
Bilingual Press / Editorial Bilingüe ISBN 978-1-939743-10-7 $ 31.50

Vol. 15
Raab, Josef, and Saskia Hertlein, eds. *Spaces – Communities – Discourses: Charting Identity and Belonging in the Americas*. 2016. 382 pp.
WVT Wissenschaftlicher Verlag Trier ISBN 978-3-86821-590-8 € 29,50
Bilingual Press / Editorial Bilingüe ISBN 978-1-939743-13-8 $ 39.50

Vol. 16
Mehring, Frank, ed. *The Mexico Diary: Winold Reiss between Vogue Mexico and Harlem Renaissance. An Illustrated Trilingual Edition with Commentary and Musical Interpretation* (includes color plates and audio CD). 2016. 244 pp.
WVT Wissenschaftlicher Verlag Trier ISBN 978-3-86821-594-6 € 29,50
Bilingual Press / Editorial Bilingüe ISBN 978-1-939743-14-5 $ 39.50

Vol. 17
Raussert, Wilfried, Brian Rozema, Yolanda Campos, and Marius Littschwager, eds. *Key Tropes in Inter-American Studies: Perspectives from the* forum for inter-american research (fiar). 2015. 374 pp.
WVT Wissenschaftlicher Verlag Trier ISBN 978-3-86821-627-1 € 29,50
Bilingual Press / Editorial Bilingüe ISBN 978-1-939743-16-9 $ 39.50

Vol. 19
Rehm, Lukas, Jochen Kemner, and Olaf Kaltmeier, eds. *Politics of Entanglement in the Americas: Connecting Transnational Flows and Local Perspectives*. 2017. 226 pp.
WVT Wissenschaftlicher Verlag Trier ISBN 978-3-86821-675-2 € 27,50
Bilingual Press / Editorial Bilingüe ISBN 978-1-939743-17-6 $ 32.50

Vol. 20

Britt Arredondo, Christopher. *Imperial Idiocy: A Reflection on Forced Displacement in the Americas*. 2017. 194 pp.

| | | |
|---|---|---|
| WVT Wissenschaftlicher Verlag Trier | ISBN 978-3-86821-706-3 | € 26,50 |
| Bilingual Press / Editorial Bilingüe | ISBN 978-1-939743-20-6 | $ 30.00 |

Vol. 21

Schemien, Alexia. *Of Virgins, Curanderas, and Wrestler Saints: Un/Doing Religion in Contemporary Mexican American Literature*. 2018. 218 pp.

| | | |
|---|---|---|
| WVT Wissenschaftlicher Verlag Trier | ISBN 978-3-86821-724-7 | € 27,50 |
| Bilingual Press / Editorial Bilingüe | ISBN 978-1-939743-22-0 | $ 32.50 |

Vol. 22

Fulger, Maria Diana. *The Cuban Post-Socialist Exotic: Contemporary U.S. American Travel Narratives about Cuba.* 2020. 266 pp.

| | | |
|---|---|---|
| WVT Wissenschaftlicher Verlag Trier | ISBN 978-3-86821-769-8 | € 32,50 |
| Bilingual Press / Editorial Bilingüe | ISBN 978-1-939743-27-5 | $ 36.00 |

Vol. 24

Kaltmeier, Olaf, Mirko Petersen, Wilfried Raussert, and Julia Roth, eds. *Cherishing the Past, Envisioning the Future. Entangled Practises of Heritage and Utopia in the Americas.* 2021. 176 pp.

| | | |
|---|---|---|
| WVT Wissenschaftlicher Verlag Trier | ISBN 978-3-86821-804-6 | € 23,50 |
| UNO University of New Orleans Press | ISBN 978-1-60801-206-0 | $ 27.50 |

Vol. 26

Raussert, Wilfried. *'What's Going On': How Music Shapes the Social.* 2021. 224 pp.

| | | |
|---|---|---|
| WVT Wissenschaftlicher Verlag Trier | ISBN 978-3-86821-811-4 | € 28,50 |
| UNO University of New Orleans Press | ISBN 978-1-60801-199-5 | $ 34.00 |

Vol. 27

Frank-Job, Barbara. *Immigration as a Process: Temporality Concepts in Blogs of Latin American Immigrants to Québec.* 2021. 138 pp.

| | | |
|---|---|---|
| WVT Wissenschaftlicher Verlag Trier | ISBN 978-3-86821-820-6 | € 20,00 |
| UNO University of New Orleans Press | ISBN 978-1-60801-215-2 | $ 24.00 |

Vol. 28

Roth, Julia. *Can Feminism Trump Populism? Right-Wing Trends and Intersectional Contestations in the Americas.* 2021. 166 pp.

| | | |
|---|---|---|
| WVT Wissenschaftlicher Verlag Trier | ISBN 978-3-86821-821-3 | € 23,00 |
| UNO University of New Orleans Press | ISBN 978-1-60801-205-3 | $ 26.00 |

Vol. 30

Buitrago Valencia, Clara. *Missionaries: Migrants or Expatriates? Guatemalan Pentecostal Leaders in Los Angeles.* 2021. 236 pp.

| | | |
|---|---|---|
| WVT Wissenschaftlicher Verlag Trier | ISBN 978-3-86821-818-3 | € 28,50 |
| UNO University of New Orleans Press | ISBN 978-1-60801-210-7 | $ 34.50 |

Vol. 31

Schwabe, Nicole. *De-Centering History Education: Creating Knowledge of Global Entanglements.* 2021. 92 pp.

| | | |
|---|---|---|
| WVT Wissenschaftlicher Verlag Trier | ISBN 978-3-86821-828-2 | € 18,00 |
| UNO University of New Orleans Press | ISBN 978-1-60801-214-5 | $ 21.00 |

Vol. 32

Manke, Albert. *Coping with Discrimination and Exclusion. Experiences of Free Chinese Migrants in the Americas in a Transregional and Diachronic Perspective.* 2021. 162 pp.

| | | |
|---|---|---|
| WVT Wissenschaftlicher Verlag Trier | ISBN 978-3-86821-829-9 | € 23,00 |
| UNO University of New Orleans Press | ISBN 978-1-60801-207-7 | $ 27.00 |

Vol. 33

Rohland, Eleonora. *Entangled Histories and the Environment? Socio-Environmental Transformations in the Caribbean, 1492-1800.* 2021. 92 pp.

| | | |
|---|---|---|
| WVT Wissenschaftlicher Verlag Trier | ISBN 978-3-86821-833-6 | € 18,00 |
| UNO University of New Orleans Press | ISBN 978-1-60801-208-4 | $ 21.00 |

Vol. 34

Kaltmeier, Olaf. *National Parks from North to South. An Entangled History of Conservation and Colonization in Argentina.* 2021. 210 pp.

| | | |
|---|---|---|
| WVT Wissenschaftlicher Verlag Trier | ISBN 978-3-86821-834-3 | € 27,50 |
| UNO University of New Orleans Press | ISBN 978-1-60801-204-6 | $ 32.50 |

Vol. 35

Raussert, Wilfried. *Off the Grid. Art Practices and Public Space.* 2021. 232 pp.

| | | |
|---|---|---|
| WVT Wissenschaftlicher Verlag Trier | ISBN 978-3-86821-835-0 | € 29,50 |
| UNO University of New Orleans Press | ISBN 978-1-60801-213-8 | $ 34.50 |

Vol. 36

Ravasio, Paola. *This Train Is Not Bound to Glory. A Study of Literary Trainscapes.* 2021. 114 pp.

| | | |
|---|---|---|
| WVT Wissenschaftlicher Verlag Trier | ISBN 978-3-86821-836-7 | € 18,00 |
| UNO University of New Orleans Press | ISBN 978-1-60801-216-9 | $ 21.00 |

Vol. 37

Schäfer, Heinrich Wilhelm. *Protestant 'Sects' and the Spirit of (Anti-)Imperialism. Religious Entanglements in the Americas.* 2021. 242 pp.

| | | |
|---|---|---|
| WVT Wissenschaftlicher Verlag Trier | ISBN 978-3-86821-855-9 | € 29,50 |
| UNO University of New Orleans Press | ISBN 978-1-60801-209-1 | $ 34.50 |